DEDICATION

I dedicate this book to God for giving me life, health, strength, guidance, faith, inspiration and motivation to help others in addition to myself. Without him, this book would not have been born. Special thanks to my family and friends for being supportive.

A very special thanks to Larry Oskin, Alan Benfield Bush, Mar Finer, Sonya Davis and Daija Howard. For contributing so much value on this special book project.

To those who have helped me build a foundation for my career my mentors Pam Perry and Ann Sieg. Thanks for impacting my life in a big way and to all of the aspiring beauty professionals who are positively impacting people lives on a daily basis.

Table of Contents

Hair$tylist Riches

The Original Beauty Salon Business Breakthrough Success Guide For Hair Stylists Who Need Inspiration On Creating An Extraordinary New Life And Business They Love

Compiled by International Best Selling Author
Charlotte Howard

ISBN-13: 978-0692670590

Charlotte Howard - Heart Centered Women Media

108 Flintlock Lane

Summerville, SC/USA 29486

www.thehairartistassociation.org

charlotte@thehairartistassociation.org

Book Cover ©2016 Charlotte Howard - Heart Centered Women Media

Book Layout ©2016 Charlotte Howard - Heart Centered Women Media

Compiled By Charlotte Howard - Founder & CEO Hair Artist Association, LLC

Ordering Information:

Quantity sales. Special discounts are available on quantity purchases by corporations, associations, and others. For details, contact the "Special Sales Department" at the address above.

INTRODUCTION

For over a decade I've been teaching hairstylists and beauty salon business experts around the world how to create fulfillment and happiness in their lives doing what they love. I am honored today to share with you how to passionately follow your dreams and create the life you deserve with confidence.

In 2011, I created the Hair Artist Association, a platform for brand new and experienced beauty industry professionals worldwide to connect and support each other. HAA is a platform created for you to build partnerships with other beauty professionals.

HAA is a platform created for you to share and discover the latest beauty salon trends, beauty salon events, beauty salon education, beauty salon products, beauty salon services, beauty salon tools, beauty salon resources, beauty salon business opportunities and beauty salon career opportunities.

HAA is a global association head quartered in Summerville, SC dedicated to engaging, inspiring and change the lives of beauty industry professionals. HAA goal is to strategically partner with beauty industry professionals, corporations and small business owners to bring you value for you to grow personally and professionally.

"Charlotte Howard is one of those rare finds: An individual with a wealth of knowledge and experience in her field who is at the same time equipped to meet people "where they are" with a soft, personal touch and help them craft solutions that are as unique as their problems might be. I have no doubt that she will continue to help strengthen hair stylists and beauty industry professionals for many years to come!" – Elizabeth Kraus, Be InPulse & 12 Months of Marketing

An Open letter from Charlotte Howard:

Dear Friend,

How much is your fulfillment and happiness worth?

Suppose you could use proven step by step strategies and support to help you create the life you deserve with confidence in record time.

Imagine what it would be like to position your service as the best solution to current and potential clients and customers.

Sounds too good to be true? Well, it isn't if you have the right connections, tools, resources and systems in place.

Think about it. Confidence is essential for winning in all areas of your life, career and business. It will help you to create the lifestyle you deserve, attract more ideal clients and customers enabling you to increase your revenue with less effort. Simply put, you would save more money and time by using the very same techniques all the top experts in the industry are using right now.

But Creating That Success Is The Hard Part…

It could take you years and can cost you a small fortune to figure out just the right combinations that make some hairstylists succeed – while others fall flat on their face.

But instead of knocking yourself out trying to come up with just the right strategies, resources, tools, connections and systems, you can now have it inside this brand new second edition of "Hair Stylist Riches".

At last! Everything you need to create an extraordinary new life and business is here.

CHAPTER 1

WHY IT'S IMPORTANT TO LOVE YOURSELF AND PUT GOD FIRST IN EVERYTHING YOU DO

There are many successful people out there who are living their life as they want to. They are working hard doing what they absolutely love to do. The most successful people are those who work toward the things they are passionate about and love. There are many reasons for this. The more you love what you do the harder you are going to work at it because you will be enjoying your work.

If you feel like you are bored with your life or not doing what you should be doing with it then it is time to make a change. There maybe obstacles or fears holding you back from accomplishing the goals you have set forth in your life. It is time to get past the obstacles and make your dreams come true.

Many people aren't quite sure what their true passion is. They want to work toward being successful as they see many other people but they just aren't sure what it is that they can do. Finding your passion is possible and it will take some deep searching within yourself. I know that if you put God first in everything you do things will work out for you. God will provide the answer for you but you must ask him. Your passion maybe right in front of you and you don't even realize it.

Every passion has the capability of making money. It is just seeing the angle you need to take to make it happen. You shouldn't sit around and avoid your passion because you don't think you could financially survive on it because you can.

Enthusiasm is what makes the difference between reaching our goals and giving up before we get started. Thomas Edison said, "If the only thing we leave our kids is the quality of enthusiasm, we will have given them an estate of incalculable value." Edison's research laboratory burned to the ground when he was 67. As the fire consumed his world-famous "invention factory," Edison told his children, "Kids, go get your mother. She'll never see another fire like this one." Edison knew that enthusiasm is the best antidote for tragedy, and it's the most powerful weapon to use in the war against procrastination.

I have learned that my level of enthusiasm has nothing to do with my feelings; my feelings wake up on a different side of the bed every day. To take control of my life, I must choose the way I feel-I can't let my feelings control me. Can you talk yourself into a positive frame of mind when you're discouraged? How do you keep yourself motivated? How do you stay focused when a job is tedious? How do you handle failure when your plan isn't going well?

- Stay away from negative people. Attitudes are contagious-negative people infect us with negative attitudes. Associate with positive thinkers; their self-confidence is contagious, too.

- Schedule difficult tasks for the time of day when your energy is highest. If you haven't determined the best time for you to tackle the day's least appealing jobs, try doing them as early as possible.

- Tackle a problem that's been a thorn in your side. When you get in the habit of making things happen, your enthusiasm goes through the roof. Inactivity is a major cause of depression and anxiety. (On the other hand, you can increase your energy level without eliminating other forces that cause procrastination; teenagers are particularly adept at expending enormous amounts of energy without getting anything done. Always remember that any technique is only effective when used as part of a total strategy.)

When you breeze through a task with particular ease and competence, make a note of the time of day. And ask yourself what other factors might have contributed to making you more productive. When you start to discover a pattern, you will have found how to operate at a higher level every day. And when you identify the time of day when you are usually most efficient, schedule some of your least enjoyable tasks for that time.

We must continue to learn new things as if we were going to live forever, while living each day as if it were the last. Telling myself that

"Today is the first day of the rest of my life" doesn't work for me. If today were the last day of my life, how would I live it? That is the question I ask myself when I must fight against the forces of procrastination.

Always remember that enthusiasm is a choice. Mark Twain said, "Do something every day that you don't want to do; this is the golden rule for acquiring the habit of doing your duty without pain."

As a hairstylist it is very important to conquer your worries, improve your work/life balance and free up some space in your life for personal/professional growth.

Does any of this sound familiar to you?

Your plate is full.

Overflowing in fact.

On any given weekend or late evening, chances are you can be found in the beauty salon working.

Have you thought about delegating? Probably you have.

Delegating enables us to have better work and life balance, to develop others, encourages teamwork, provides a richer array of perspectives on any given project, and, utilizes everyone's skills and talents more efficiently.

So, let's take a look at the reasons why we so often tend not to ask others to contribute in delivering the work we do.

- It won't get done, or it won't get done correctly
- I'll just have to nag until it gets done
- They are really busy too
- I don't have help
- No one else can do it
- I want to be recognized for my contributions

These are all perfectly good reasons for not wanting to delegate. But in this instance, you can "have your cake and eat it too!"

Do you want a healthy work and life balance?

Do you want your life back?

You can delegate, and the work will get done. And, here's the kicker-you will be a better beauty salon professional for it! I've seen it over and over again a salon manager drops more tasks on the hairstylist, mumbles a few quick words about getting something done and is off and running, ready to tackle 10 other things demanding his or her attention.

The result?

It doesn't get done, or not correctly, or not the salon manager's (unspoken) specifications. This then, only serves to validate the salon manager's belief that there is no real help available.

Does this sound familiar?

Let's take this example then, and explore how you can confidently delegate, and improve the outcome for all involved!

- It's better to give too much information, than too little.

Remember, this individual to whom you are delegating may not have been privy to discussions/meetings in which you have been involved. What are the key pieces of information they will need in order to get it done, and done well the first time? Identify those, then share them.

- Are all the pieces to the puzzle available?

What reports, materials, or contacts can help the individual complete the task?

Are they accessible? Share these resources. Also inquire as to whether or not the person to whom you are delegating has the skills or competencies required to successfully accomplish the task.

- Identify a clear timeframe. By when do you want to see the deliverable? When identifying a deadline, ensure sufficient time for making adjustments as needed.

- Identify what the actual deliverable should look, feel or be like.

For example, if you're expecting three new clients to be serviced rather than a one client, say so. Share your vision of the deliverable.

- As appropriate, delegate to provide a development opportunity for someone else. If you do, your boss will not only have "dedicated" on his list of your positive qualities, but be assured "team player" and "great manager" will be there as well.

Coaching and training can help you improve your skills and confidence in managing your workload, as well as in developing others. Don't be shy about requesting the support you'd like to receive from your employer.

If you need another staff member, because you truly do not have an individual to share the work with, make a case for it and request one. If you would like to develop these skills, request support from a coach, or find a development program to meet your specific needs. After all, the quality of your life depends on it!

You can't expect to hit a target if you don't have a target in the first place. You must set hairstylist business goals in order to effectively achieve anything. Preferably, your goals should be written down.

When framing your hairstylist business goals, there are five basic things to consider, as we learned in grade school, called the "5 W"s. The first to ask yourself is the "what" question. "What is my hairstylist business goal in this situation?" and "What do I hope to gain from this hairstylist business goal?" for example.

The second question is the "why" question. "Why am I interested in accomplishing this hairstylist business goal?"

The third is the "when" question, as in, "when do you plan to meet this hairstylist business goal?"

You may need to ask "Who will I need to get help from?" This is a motivating question to get you to think about planning your hairstylist business goal. And the last of the five is the "where" question. The where question can be "Where am at right now in relation to accomplishing my hairstylist business goal?" But there is another important question to ask yourself in addition to all of this.

Once you have answer the 5W's, the next important question in hairstylist business goal planning is: how. How are you going to accomplish your hairstylist business goal? This is where the real planning of your hairstylist business goal begins to shape.

Setting hairstylist business goals and telling your subconscious mind what you want to change does not involve magical incantations; there's not just one right way to do it, but there are some pitfalls to avoid:

1. Avoid vague wording - One characteristic of the subconscious mind that can really be irritating is the way it takes everything so literally. That sounds Ok – maybe even obvious – until you take a look at how sloppy our language really is.

2. Be positive. Always try to use positive wording for your hairstylist business goals. This can be difficult, especially in those situations where you are trying to quit old habits or getting rid of something. If you absolutely have to use a negatively formulated hairstylist business goal, go ahead, but try for the positive approach first.

3. Use "I". In your hairstylist business goals, address yourself as "I," not "you". Say "I will . . ." Your aims are a conversation with yourself, your own subconscious mind. It is part of you.

4. Be visual. Your subconscious mind understands pictures more readily than words, but you have to communicate with it through words, to some extent. Therefore, the trick in getting your subconscious mind to understand what changes you are trying to affect is to build pictures. Make them as vivid and clear as possible with lots of description.

5. Make it Personal. Use language and images which reflect your own experience. We all have our own memories and experiences of the world, and speak to ourselves in our own language. Express your hairstylist business goals in your own words and use images you are familiar with.

Get the language right on your hairstylist business goal planning and you will be fired up with enthusiasm with a clear idea on how to achieve your hairstylist business goals.

The purpose of this book is to help you find your real passion within you and create the life you deserve. If you want to lead a successful career in the beauty industry. Always remember to put god first in all you do. Repeat these success affirmations every day and abide by them every day. You will continue to be blessed and prosperous just like god wants everyone to be.

And whatever you do, do it heartily, as to the Lord and not to men, knowing that from the Lord you will receive the reward of the inheritance; for you serve the Lord Christ. - Colossians 3:23-24

Now faith is the substance of things hoped for,the evidence of things not seen. -Hebrews 11:1

Now to Him who is able to do exceedingly abundantly above all that we ask or think, according to the power that works in us.. - Ephesians 3:20

For we are His workmanship, created in Christ Jesus for good works, which God prepared beforehand that we should walk in them. -Ephesians 2:10

The blessings of the Lord makes one rich, And He adds no sorrow with it. -Proverbs 10:22

Therefore I say to you, whatever things you ask when you pray, believe that you receive them, and you will have them. -Mark 11:24

And you will seek Me and find Me, when you search for Me with all your heart.

-Jeremiah 29:13

Those who are planted in the house of the Lord shall flourish in the courts of our God.

-Psalm 92:13

Wisdom is the principal thing; Therefore get wisdom. And in all your getting, get understanding. -Proverbs 4:7

Here are Eight proven ideas for building your confidence so you can magnetically attract new clients :

1. Use Music

One of the simplest tricks for helping yourself to both take action and feel more confident: Creating your own inspiring musical playlist, and playing it whenever appropriate. (Athletes know this secret and use music all the time, while training at the gym.)

Just as sad music in minor keys can help us process feelings when life deals blows like relationship breakups, so can energizing music or inspiring music actually raise our confidence level to the point where we take action.

Choose your own favorite "theme song". It will automatically boost your confidence whenever you hear it.

2. Dress for Success

This doesn't mean putting on a formal business suit. It does mean dressing in a way that boosts your self-confidence and makes you feel good about yourself.

Don't try to copy your ideal client or niche influencer unless that's a look you totally relate to. It's more important to dress in a way that makes you feel you have already achieved your top goal. If you see yourself with gypsy-style earrings and East Indian cotton skirts in many colors and layers, go for it. If you see yourself as edgy and trendy, go for it. If you see yourself in tweeds and Arran sweaters, wear them! And take note of how it makes you feel, when you dress for success.

Change your hairstyle. Buy those shoes you've been wistfully drooling over. Don't worry about what other people think. Wearing what makes you feel successful and confident will attract the right client— for you.

3. Adopt a Mantra and Live By It

In the 1999 movie, "Galaxy Quest", an entire civilization bases its core values on a cheesy TV sci-fi show from Earth. They take the series hero's glib motto, "Never give up; never surrender" to new heights— and achieve peace within a warring society before teaming up with earthmen to defeat a super villain.

This is what happens when you adopt a mantra, motto or slogan—and live by it.

"Never give up; never surrender" is a great motto, when you are trying to build new habits that increase your confidence.

4. Start Small

Do you have a big change to make? Don't wait for the "right time"— start small. For example, if you want a new office but can't afford it, try buying a new piece of furniture or an accessory for your office that will make your life easier—like a bookshelf; or even just a shelf. Or a new lamp, to reduce the chronic eyestrain you suffer. Or even just some flowers because you deserve them!

When you start to surround yourself with things that signify success or make life easier, you are sending yourself a strong message - "I CAN have this in my life! I deserve this!"

5. Make Confidence a Habit

Contrary to what others might think, no one is born with supreme self-confidence. It has to be learned. And it CAN be learned.

So consciously work on changing your habits. Take actions you need to take, change negative self-talk to realistic and more positive talk, and actively adopt the attitude of what you define as a successful person.

Confidence is not only for the lucky few who "succeed". Anyone can have it—all you have to do is make it a habit.

6. Realize Your Clients Need—and Want—Your Services

Instead of expending energy trying to attract new clients, focus on the ones you already have. They already trust you. They have "bought" from you and they are still coming back for more.

Make sure you meet and exceed their expectations. Be proactive. Anticipate their needs at the next level. Provide aides, extras and resources at the right time. Go over their notes, think about them. Empathize with their problems and dreams.

If you do this—if you treat your existing clients as if they are diamonds —you will automatically attract the same type of client who already wants your services.

7. Know Your Own Value

The most confident people are those who know their own worth: What their time is worth, what their life experience and expertise is worth and what their services are worth.

Track your time. Look over your achievements and credentials. Read your client testimonials and emails. Identify the area where you help people make the biggest shifts.

Realizing how truly unique and valuable you are to clients can give you the confidence to set a realistic and healthy value on your services... so you can stop over-delivering and under-charging, and have the confidence to know you deserve your fees.

8. Add Achievement Acknowledgement to Practicing Gratitude

By now you've probably heard the phrase "attitude of gratitude" a gazillion times, and as a coach, you probably know all about the technique of waking up every morning and listing things you are grateful for, before starting your day.

This is a great practice—but add to it three things that you do as a beauty industry professional that you are proud of. You can make it about the past, the present, what you are going to do today or what you achieved yesterday.

2 CHAPTER
HOW TO USE YOUR POWERFUL HAIR ARTISTRY TO BUILD YOUR CREDIBILITY

Hairstyling has become one of the most demanded services under beauty care and personal grooming. With more and more people showing enthusiasm in experimenting with their looks, the need for professional hairstylists has increased extensively. Many people interested in the fashion industry have taken up hairstyling professionally to help people enhance the way they look. If you are someone who is interested in the hair business, you will need to join a good cosmetology school to get the best hair stylist degree. Once you become an expert at hair cutting, weaving, coloring and styling hair in the best way possible. There is a lot more that you need to learn once you graduate if you want to run your hair salon business effectively.

Like any other industry, the beauty and grooming industry has quite a lot of competition. This means that to survive in this industry, you will need to use your expertise to build your credibility and attract customers to your salon. When it comes to your hair business, it is only a good clientele base that will help you own a successful salon business. A good marketing strategy is one of the most important keys to becoming a successful hairstylist. During bad economic times people would still visit a hair salon in order to look good and feel better.

Increasing your client base or keeping your client loyal to you might seem overwhelming. However, if you have an effective marketing plan, this is not really difficult to accomplish. Here are some basic marketing ideas that you can use to increase your customer base:

- The best way to build your customer base is to keep in constant contact with your customers. As a matter of fact, it is recommended that you create a beauty club where you enroll members. You may want to offer special deals and offers to the members of your club. This will ensure that you have a loyal client base.

- When you begin your hair salon business, you can even send a flyer to everyone you know to make them aware of your hair styling business. You can even offer a free first appointment or any special deal to invite more customers.

- With hair salon businesses, it is extremely important to build a good rapport with your clients to keep them coming back to you. You can maintain a database of your clients with the birthday, anniversary, etc to call them on these special occasions and offer them a discount. You can even have festival offers to attract new customers.

While it is true that your hair salon business will grow by word of mouth, you cannot solely depend on this source to stay in business. Planning your marketing strategy is essential to have a successful hair salon business.

A hairstylist is a highly talented person who has the skill to enhance the looks of a person by styling his or her hair in the best possible manner. Hairstylists have the power to change so many lives with the talents they possess. With a cosmetology license you have the power of creating over 100 careers in the beauty industry. Hairstylists like doctors are the only other profession that has a license to touch people.

People in today's times are looking at creating those everlasting impressions that help them become more confident at whatever they do. A good personality is an important aspect for building confidence and the right beauty treatment can do wonders in creating an impressive personality. Hair styling is one of the basic and perhaps the most important of beauty treatments that can instantly transform anyone from being a plain Jane to a style diva. Considering this fact, the demand for hairstylist has increased largely across the world.

Many hairstylists operate as independent contractors. This gives them the leverage to serve clients belonging to different places, age groups, etc and offer their services for various purposes. It could be to style the hair of a bride or the bridesmaids for a wedding or to be a hairstylist for a Hollywood celebrity for a movie or a public event – a freelance hairstylist definitely has a wider customer base. A majority of hairstylists operate as self-employed professionals. The biggest advantage to a freelance hairstylist is the fact that he or she takes home all the money as well as the credit for the styling services he or she provides.

While the fact remains that a freelance hair stylist has more professional freedom and better chances of gaining popularity, it might be quite difficult to win the trust and confidence of the clients. If you are a freelance hairstylist, you might wonder how to overcome this problem. In order to promote yourself against the established hair salons, you will need to have a strong marketing plan. One of the easiest and the most recommended methods that you can use as an independent hairstylist is social media and internet marketing.

Social networking and social media sites provide amazing opportunities for a freelance hairstylist to promote his or her skill. An independent hairstylist can create his or her professional profile and post pictures of the hair styling created on social sites. This will help in promoting and marketing his or her skill quite effectively. If you are an independent hairstylist, you will be quite amazed at the response you receive from social media marketing. While you can improve your visibility through internet and social media; you can also promote your services by offering your potential customers the benefit of price and convenience.

A freelance hairstylist is also in a better position to develop a personal bond with the customers. By being in constant touch with the current and prospective clients, a freelance hairstylist can easily and conveniently become highly successful.

Niche salon marketing is another great way for you to build your credibility. It involves focusing and marketing a particular salon niche. The marketing concept has numerous benefits. You not only attract clients who have an interest in your salon but also those who know where their particular needs will be met. Thus your consumers can view your salon as trustworthy to give them what they want and desire. Not only do you get customers that want what you have to offer but also increase the credibility of your salon.

A narrow and easily-defined niche can have a great impact by making your salon an attracting salon. When you try to be all things to people it makes it hard to be identified. The target market can identify you fast. Target salon marketing can help in writing up a precise and compelling message that can pierce the heart of that market and that market alone.

You need to identify a target market

You can target your potential market by styles, region, socioeconomic status and gender. There are numerous groups of small people with identifiable needs, buying habits and jobs. Know where you can best serve clients and look to position yourself. Considerations when identifying your target market include competition, problem, solution, type of customers and customer base. You can also consider if the target group has the money to afford your services.

Specifically-branded service

After identifying a niche, you can now go ahead and create a specific-branded service to attract clients. The precise service sets you apart from your competition because you will not have to give clients the usual bland response when asked about your services.

Market where your niche market will look

If your target market is more likely to see your advertisement on television, then it is better to advertise on TV. Choose an advertising medium that your target market uses the most. You can also market in the Internet, radio, newspapers and magazines.

Give the right message

Your beauty salon marketing efforts should include a well-crafted message that will be absorbed by the target market. The message should address the problem and provide the solution. Address a unique need that is valuable to your clients.

Set a good price

A good price for value is always attractive. Make sure your target market can afford your unique service. You can base the price depending on the value you give your clients. While you are at it, attract salon clients with discounts and offers.

This industry is so full of rewards but not everyone is taking advantage of the power of beauty. If you are not a happy person in this industry that is a choice you are making. You have full control over your life and the decisions that you make. There are many factors which people measure happiness. Some people think money is happiness however they may be absolutely miserable with what they do on a daily basis to make their money.

You might look at people who have absolutely everything and you strive to be like them. These things may be wealth, possessions, status, or even the position you hold at work. These things don't create happiness. Happiness is a choice.

There are many people who have wealth and a high status who are completely miserable. They may be lonely, divorced and more. Happiness comes from within, as a hairstylist helping your client will first start from within.

Everyone seeks happiness in their own way.

3 CHAPTER
HOW TO MASTER YOUR HAIR ARTISTRY EVEN IF YOU ARE BRAND NEW

As a new hair stylist, you need to come with strategies to ensure you get clients into your salon. This is because the salon business is tricky as mostly you get to deal with 'repeat' customers due to the regularity within which the service is utilized. On the other hand, you want to build your customer base and beat the already established competition. Here are tips to help you get customers into your salon; Customer or Client Satisfaction and Connection Ensure that you give your clients the best service that they deserve.

Connect and communicate with them to know how they like their hair done and if they can book an appointment with you. In the modern world we live in, they might be having a busy schedule and exposing such details to you will make you aware how best you can allocate them time. Moreover, get to know if your target customers are people with big budgets or thrifty such that you can come up with a way to tailor your services to suit them. Also, let the experience be a pleasant one. Eventually, they will leave the premises happy and most probably refer more clients to you.

Internet marketing is very important for salons. The majority of people use the internet nowadays to shop. Similarly, place your ads in the mostly used sites. Social media platforms have become attractive sites to market products and services. Similarly, you can market your salon in one of the social sites and inform your target market of any new hair styles, special offers and any gifts or deals that you may be offering. However, ensure that you don't compromise on your services as this will most likely end up on the social site. Social events Use social functions to promote your salon.

Community events like sports, holiday parties, tea parties, barbeques, trade shows and others can be used to build a client base. Have a business telephone contact number that the clients can use to inquire on your services and any special offers you might be having. Moreover, teach your staff on proper telephone etiquette to reveal to the client the professionalism involved in the business. Also, keep the staff updated when you change prices on hairstyles or when you have new offers. SWOT Analysis SWOT means Strength, Weakness, Opportunity and Threat.

The competition is your main threat, more so being a new place of business or stylist. However, you might be a threat to your business if your services are not up to standard or the professionalism is questionable. On the other hand, get to know your strength over your competitors and how you can build on it. On the other hand, your weak areas will make the clients prefer the competition, hence work on it, and the competitions' weakness will bring clients to you. Similarly, get to know it and compare yourself with the competition. Keep in touch with your clients Ensure that you keep in touch with the clients you already have.

Remember, it costs more to recruit a new client than to bring back a strayed one. Moreover, you build a relationship with your clients who can be a good source of information on how the competition is. This can be achieved by sending birthday cards, thank you notes, promotion gear as well as regular emails to update them on any changes in your services. You can also market your salon by rewarding your regular clients with discounts on skin care products or offering gifts to those who have spent a given amount in your salon in a given period. Still, ensure that most of the services offered in your salon complement each other such that its possible for a client to get a massage, manicure and pedicure, facial therapy and shop for skin care products on top of having her hair done. Generally, clients prefer a one-stop-shop for most of what they need.

What really inspires and engages you?

This question may be a little difficult to answer but you may find the answer after you finish the rest of the questions. However, you need to be very clear about where you get your inspiration from. What are the types of things you find engaging and exciting in the beauty industry?

If you couldn't fail, what would you do?

Many people don't do things because they are afraid to fail or they have failed in the past. If there is something that you would do for sure if you knew there isn't a chance whatsoever of failing in the beauty industry what would that be?

If you were forced to start over again, what would you do?

Many people find themselves in situations where they are not doing as they wish they were in the beauty industry. They go to work because they have to, not enjoying a single day of it. If you started over again would you take advantage of the new beginning or would you go back to where you are? What would you do?

If money wasn't an issue, what would you do?

Many people have dreams they wish to pursue in the beauty industry but they never attempt to move forward with the dreams because they cannot afford to get started. Think of what you would love to do if you had the money to do it. This can be anything.

What is your biggest dream?

If you have a big dream, what is it? There must be something you really want to do in the beauty industry that you dream about. Think about this one thing and focus on it.

What is the biggest barrier stopping you from following your dream?

Name all of the things that have caused you to not follow your big dreams. These things could be people who do not support you, money, fears, and other things. There are many different types of barriers which can be overcome. You might not see opportunity or success with your dreams in the beauty industry or you may fear that people would make fun of you. You might not even be skilled and lack talent. These could be barriers causing you not to move forward.

What passion are you afraid of owning or admitting?

Many people have dreams and passions of being in the beauty industry but they are afraid to talk about out of fear of being made fun of by other people. You might think your passion is silly to other people. What is this one thing?

As a child, what did you really want to be?

Did you have dreams of becoming a beauty industry professional as a child and it didn't turn out quite as expected? Do you still wonder what it would have been like if you did follow your dreams as a child? If you had the opportunity, would you follow this dream today?

If you were going to die in the near future, what would you regret not doing?

Many people have regrets when they realize they are going to die real soon. It is often too late for many people to go back and change the things they missed out on. They would have lived their lives completely differently if they had the chance. If a doctor told you that you hadn't any time left but a few weeks, then what would your regrets be? What would you want to do before your time was up?

Now that you have answered these questions you should have a good idea if the beauty industry will be your dream path. Knowing these things is very important. It will help you to shape the passion driven beauty career you desire.

Your passion comes from inside and if you truly love what you are doing then this will come naturally for you. You will take pride in your work and if you design wigs then you won't send a low quality wig out to a customer because you will be passionate about the quality. This is because you will own it and your name will be on it.

In order for you to become a master at your hair artistry you will have to learn all the aspects of the business. Retailing products is very important in a salon selling business. Aside from the earning that you will get from the salon services that you will be giving your clients, you can also make a lot of money from the product sales. It can really make a difference per month if you do well in salon selling of products. Before you can become successful with it, there are some tips that you can follow.

Observe the Business

If you are the manager or the owner of a salon then you should know the way your salon selling goes. You should know which products are selling well and which ones aren't. For the ones which are selling really well, then you might need more stocks for those kinds of products. For those which aren't, then you might need to do something about it. Maybe, a more presentation is needed.

Provide Sampling

Salon products manufacturers offer samples. You better get them for your clients to try. Anyway, if your client likes the product then they would probably buy from you. You can also get your stylists try the product themselves so that they can have a good idea about the product. How can they recommend the product to your clients or use the product the right way if they haven't tried it in the first place.

Make the Products Visible to the Client

Make the product visible and touchable to your clients. You can display some products in the checkout area or in front of the client's waiting lounge. This strategy works to any retailing and marketing. They should have the freedom to smell and to touch the products. Of course, you should also do the talking. Tell them how good the product is and you can also tell them about the downsides of the product. This way, you can get their trust because you are not directly selling to them.

Suggestions Only

Do not tell them to buy the product. Tell them that the product is good for the kind of hairstyle they have. Just suggest and do not directly sell. Your clients would probably trust your salon selling technique if you just suggest. It is a fact that people trust those who don't sell but those who build a connection.

Recommend the Product

After working on a client, you can suggest a product that could maintain or enhance her or his current looks. If one or two of your clients buy from you each day, then you would probably have a fruitful month.

The salon selling tips that you can find above aren't complete. All of the tips above are just ideas which are proven and tested however they might not work with you. It cannot be avoided because there are a lot of factors that should be considered. In any business, ideas should be applied to test whether it works or not. For a successful salon business, you should try some ideas that might work with you and create your own style and approach. This way, you can surely become a better business venture and make some more money out from your salon selling business.

4 CHAPTER
HOW TO BUILD YOUR HAIR ARTISTRY PLATFORM USING THE POWER OF SOCIAL MEDIA

As a hairstylist, it is in the best of your abilities to provide excellent service to your clients and educate them with the best products as well as services to suit their needs not yours. With that in mind, you will want to be everywhere possible to help as many people as possible.

The internet has been a great source for this and one of the best ways I know to reach new clients and existing clients is through social networks like facebook, linkedin, and twitter. We can't however, forget the major video application site like youtube which will get you plenty of exposure for your business.

Our generation will definitely imprint an unforgettable mark in history. Computer technology has been innovated and improved. Surfing the internet is now one of the pastime activities of the youth and not only that, people of different walks of life do enjoy surfing the net.

What are the activities that people enjoy in surfing the world wide web? Actually, there are lot of things to do in front of your internet connected computer. You can now have your reports done and submit to your heads in no time at all; blogging is also good where you can have your personalized blogs and let the world learn updates about you. Not only that, you can also communicate with your relatives abroad and see them moving inside your computer monitor. Amazing right!

Internet can also link you to your old friends. There's nothing impossible with internet nowadays. If you have any concern on anything under the sun, you are just keywords away from them. You just have to browse the proper keywords and there you go, you will be brought in the topic you have chosen.

FACEBOOK

In meeting and connecting with your old friends, there are social networking websites that could be of help. One of those is the

Facebook. Facebook, previously known as The facebook is a free-access social networking website that is operated and privately owned by Facebook, Inc. Users are asked to identify themselves through the group organization they have setup. Networks are organized by city, school, workplace and region to link one with other people.

In Facebook, you can send personal messages and upload pictures to update your colleagues, relatives and old friends to know your whereabouts. Mark Zuckerberg founded the Facebook while studying at Harvard University. At first, it was exclusive to the students of the said university but later on was expanded to other colleges and expanded further to all the university students and finally to anyone aged 13 and over. As of now, there is 175 million users worldwide and keeps on multiplying each day.

A lot of comparison has been made with Facebook. Media often compares the said social networking website to MySpace but the major difference of the two is actually the level of customization. The other site allows its users to decorate their profile layouts using CSS or Cascading Style Sheets while Facebook only allows plain text.

Facebook has a number of features such as the following:

- Wall – this is a space on the user's profile page allowing friends to post messages for the other users to see

- Pokes – this feature allows users to send virtual "pokes" to each other

- Photos – this feature allows the sure to upload photos and organize them in albums

- Status – allows users to inform their friends of their whereabouts and actions

- News Feed – it appears on the user's profile page and appears on every user's homepage and emphasizes information regarding the profile changes, upcoming events and birthdays related to the friends of the user.

- Facebook Notes – this one allows tags and images that are embeddable

- Chat – users can now communicate with friends using this feature

- Gifts – you can now send virtual gifts to your friends and these will appear on the profile of the recipient.
- Marketplace – this features allows the users to post free classifieds

TWITTER

Twitter is a social networking and micro – blogging service allowing the users to send and read updates of the other users. These are text – based posts of up to 140 characters in length and is called tweets. Twitter users can receive updates via SMS and RSS or through applications such as TwitterMobile, Twinkle, Facebook, Tweetie, Twitterific, Twidget and Feedalizr.

A word or phrase prefixed with a # sign is called hashtags and this may be used in tagging tweeter messages. This enables tweets on a particular subject to be found by simply searching the net for their common hashtags, provided that the user tagged their tweets.

Number of twitter users keeps on increasing and the registration of new members is evident on its everyday records. Features of Twitter have been also improving. And with Twitter, you might as well create a constant communication with your old friends, classmates and colleagues.

YOUTUBE

Youtube is video sharing website that allows users to upload, view and share videos to their person of interest. In February 2005, Youtube was founded by the three former employees of PayPal. It was bought by Google Inc in November, 2006 and has become subsidiary of Google.

You have to register if you want to upload videos but you can watch video clips even if you don't have Youtube account. Accounts of the registered users are called "channels."

Unregistered users can watch the videos, while registered users are permitted to upload an unlimited number of videos. Accounts of registered users are called "channels."

There are also some restrictions and these are included in the terms of service of Youtube. Uploading of pornographic videos and violating copyrights are strictly prohibited. Registered users over the age of 18 are the only people allowed to watch potentially offensive clips.

As a registered user, you also have the rights to post your comments on the videos or spam them. Other users may reply your posts or tag them as good or bad comment. Youtube is doing a great job in providing educational, romantic and informative video clips.

LINKEDIN

LinkedIn is a business oriented social networking site founded in December 2002 and launched in May 2003. As of today, it has 35 million registered users and is still multiplying everyday.

LinkedIn allows its users to maintain a list of the contact details of the people they know and trust in their chosen field. People included in your list are called Connections and you can invite anyone to become a connection.

List of connections can be used in number of ways:

- You've got to know more people and learn things from each of your connection. The connection of their connections which are called the second degree connections can be extended further to another set of termed as third degree connections.

- You can find jobs and opportunities in doing business because someone in your connections will recommend you.

- People looking for employees can list and post their jobs and search for potential candidates from the pool of applicants.

- Job seekers can review the profile of the hiring individual and determine which of their existing contacts can introduce them.

The feature LinkedIn Answers is similar to Google Answers and Yahoo! Answers because just like the two, it also allows users to ask questions and the community to answer those. This feature is free. Its only difference from the two is that the questions here are potentially more business – like and the identity of the person asking and posting comments is known.

Other feature called LinkedIn Groups allows users to set up new business relationships by letting you join alumni, industry, professional and other relevant groups. The newest feature is the LinkedIn Polls which is still in alpha.

Mobile version of the site is launched in February 2008 and is available in six (6) languages: Chinese, French, German, Spanish, Japanese and English.

Facebook, Twitter, Youtube and LinkedIn are just four of the interesting websites we can visit when surfing net. Knowing that there is a bond linking you to the world is something exciting and fabulous.

Fantastic, isn't it? That's what the magic of technology does.

How to Strategically Attract Beauty Salon Clients And Customers Online

Beauty salon business marketing is not for the faint of heart, but if you've been in marketing for more than two seconds, you know that. Marketing your business is dependent on doing some key factors well and these things can make or break a beauty salon business in this dog eat dog world we live in. Competition is fierce and understanding how to make the most from your web pages is tricky.

Here are five necessary steps to get ahead of the game!

1.**Create a Marketing Plan** – A detailed marketing plan is crucial to success. You don't want to leave something to chance. It should be well thought out. Map out every marketing element, and how you intend to make it happen. At the very least, it ought to paint broad strokes to success.

2.**Social Media Marketing** – Not just a time waster! Social media is often an enormous source of website traffic and new business. According to MediaBistro.com, 91 percent of experienced social marketers see improved website traffic due to social media campaigns and 79 percent are generating more quality leads.

3.**Build a Mailing List** – MarketingProfs.com reported emails averages a ROI (return on investment) of $40 for every $1 spent. This far outweighs keyword ads ($17) and banner ads ($2). Don't be fooled into thinking collecting and building an email list is dead. If you fail to build a list, you are failing to build your business! You just cannot afford to leave such a large source of potential profits to your competition.

4.**Video Marketing** – Connect to all the local traffic that's out there trying to find your business. Video marketing in this space is a relatively untapped vein, and having a quick video advertising your wares on page one of Google can result in tons of traffic and authority coming your way! According to the research company Forrester, any given video stands about a 50x better chance of appearing on the first page of Google than any given text page.

5.**Gain a Mobile Presence** – Microsoft reports that by 2014 mobile browsing will overtake desktop browsing. If your company does not have a mobile presence, you will become invisible. This means your beauty salon business's website better start optimizing for mobile users and it had better do it quickly. Right now, the numbers are encroaching on the 50 percent mark. Are you prepared?

Don't Make the Mistake of Going It Alone!

No one is a superhero and you don't have to be. The world of online marketing is constantly changing and evolving. You need to learn what is working now, learn from the best, and hire the best outsourcing you can find. In the end, it'll pay off substantially!

Why Won't Your Beauty Salon Customers Open Your Email

Improving the email open rates of your existing list is very high in the list of how you can boost your bottom line easily. It's far easier to market to a person that has done business with you than to acquire a new beauty salon customer, and requires not nearly as much work as you might think.

With an industry average of around 27.4 percent, it's important have an understanding of your open rates, and the way you can enhance them. Toward that end, here are 10 top tips for enhancing your email open rates.

1.**Create something worth reading** - No doubt, the easiest way to have your email opened is to write something your readers can't wait to get more of.

2.**Don't' write War and Peace** - No one has enough time in their own day, and long emails that drift about and don't deliver on the promise are one way to keep them from opening again. Also, make sure you make use of optimum sending times.

3.**Build great subject lines** - This is actually the most significant factor in whether or not your email gets opened. Take your time to write great subject lines.

4.**Use your first line effectively** - Closely connected is the first line, part of which is visible in their inbox. This too is valuable real estate, and don't allow yours to be filled with things like "If you don't see any images in this message…"

5.**Give them what they really want!** - Make sure you make an effort to provide solutions.

6.**Offer deals and savings** - Everyone wants a great deal, and email is an excellent way to communicate any deals or specials your business is offering.

7.**Be the authority** - We always have something to learn, and if you are able to position yourself as somebody who offers something worthwhile for your readers, your open rates will flourish.

8.**Be entertaining** - Don't be StatMan. Don't be scared to inject humor, wit, and a little controversy on occasion.

9.**Make your "From" line recognizable** - Having your company name or the person who is branded as the sender imparts trust.

10. **Resend your unopens** - An easy action to take, taking the time to resend to your unopened email is a simple way to increase your open rates.

Don't Be The Last to Know What Your Beauty Salon Clients And Customers Want

Learning what your current and potential clients and customers really think about you can be both a fearsome and instructive thing. Doesn't it only make sense to locate any problem areas or holes in your customer service you're not aware of? The best way to obtain this type of info is to just ask them! Using a thoughtful customer survey can be a super tool to help you learn answers to questions you didn't know you had!

So why ask at all?

The main incentive for a client or customer survey is to head off problems before they become part of your reputation, and discover tips on how to strengthen your service or products. Most of the time, we never learn about a dissatisfied client or customer: they'll just look somewhere else.

CustomerThink.com has found that more than half of consumers have experienced issues and complaints with the goods and services they've purchased. Having a survey helps you find and correct mistakes that can be the difference between hanging onto a client and customer or not.

What kind of questions work best?

Make sure you have a clear objective to your surveys, and that you pose questions that require more than ticking a box, or assigning a number to your query. Avoid "Yes" or "No" questions. Allow them to expand on their experience and opinions. (This can often be a good way to collect beauty salon testimonials!)

How exactly should you hold the survey?

There a variety of ways to conduct a survey. However, if possible, the most effective way seems to be via an online survey, thus giving the respondent a good chance to think about and form well thought-out answers, something that may not occur via a phone call or personal contact. Look at offering an incentive for filling out your survey, and try to be timely as to when you send it. If you're new to this, consider using a company who specializes in this type of data collection, such as SurveyMonkey.

However you achieve it, getting a read on how your clients and customers view your beauty salon business is invaluable data to have.

5 Common Social Media Mistakes Beauty Salons Make and How to Avoid Them

Social media marketing for your beauty salon business is tough enough without shooting yourself in the foot. Self-induced social faux pas are easy to commit, and difficult to overcome. Social media is not only necessary to include, but important to get right! While some 74 percent of brand marketers saw an increase in website traffic after spending just 6 hours per week on social media, whereas another 83 percent have deserted a purchase after a bad or non-existent customer service experience. (Creotivo.com)

So to help you ward off the mistakes that might be looming in your social media marketing, listed here are five social media mistakes your beauty salon needs to be sure to avoid!

1. **No engagement with your people -**This is "social media". Be sure to ask questions, share humorous anecdotes (relevant) and by all means, ask for their thoughts. They will gladly give them to you, and you can now use this data in your beauty salon business.

2. **Lacking excitement or passion -** If you're not excited about your brand, it's likely to be very difficult to get anyone else excited about it, either. Communicate this in your postings, and in your campaigns. Everybody wants to create a buzz about our beauty salon businesses, but it starts with you!

3. **Constant promotion -** No one wants to be constantly pitched to, and there is no place this is more true than in social media. Once you've developed a relationship and trust, it's going to be much easier to insert the sporadic (soft) selling message.

4. **Not responding to clients and customers -** Sometimes beauty salon companies are so occupied either touting themselves or their services, they totally ignore or miss potential and current clients and customers posting their concerns, questions or complaints on these very platforms! What goodwill or brand awareness you have can be destroyed very quickly by ignoring your customer service opportunities!

5. **No coherent social media strategy -** Lacking, or not knowing why, you're using social media is a recipe for floundering, and wasting a great deal of time and money. Furthermore, not every beauty business is well-suited to every platform but most of them are, so give this some thought.

We'll leave you with a link to a great demonstration of what NOT to do! In an example that's being shared widely, (much to their chagrin) the food site Epicurious. After the recent Boston marathon bombing, they sent out these unfortunate tweets.

15 Homepage Sins That Might Be Costing Your Beauty Salon Business Sales

Sometimes it's about what you don't do as much as it is what you do. This can ring extremely true in regards to your beauty salon business website. There are lots of issues that can send visitors screaming into cyberspace to get away from these grievous errors. Let's find out if any one of these sound familiar to you.

1. **No clear objective** – According to DinkumInteractive.com you've got about 4 seconds to convey what your website is about before they bail.

2. **Not making the content scannable** – We read in chunks, if you can't scan your page and get the gist of it in a few seconds, you might turn off a substantial percentage of your visitors!

3. **Not being mobile ready** – Mobile is no longer an extra, as according to Google half of all online traffic is mobile.

4. **Not using videos on your website** – Just about everyone has video cameras in our phones–so there's no justification for not using video on your beauty salon business website!

5. **No updated, quality content** – If your content articles are from Bush's first term, it's no surprise they're fleeing! Also no fancy fonts or ridiculously long pages.

6. **Hard-to-find contact information** – Make certain we can get in touch with you if we want to!

7. **Not collecting emails or newsletter signups** – You do plan to be in your beauty salon business for the long haul, right?

8. **Not utilizing Meta tags on your beauty salon website** – In particular the title and description tags. These can help you to get indexed and ranked in the search engines.

9. **No social sharing buttons** – Social media is a substantial part of search engine optimization now, and you want to make your content shareable.

10. **No or poor Calls-to-Action** – You want an action from your visitors; ask for it!

11. **No clear site navigation** – Don't use drop down menus, and make certain every page on your beauty salon website includes a link back to the home page.

12. **Not optimizing your images** – Make sure to use the ALT and TITLE tags for any images or videos you use.

13. **Flash** – Besides being hard for Google to read, it can be overly annoying to your visitors!

14. **No strategy to measure your progress** – Do you have some form of web metrics measuring your stats? If not, you're flying blind.

15. **"Intro" pages** – These are simply an obstacle to your content. You really want to go there? (I'm looking at you, fancy beauty salon business owners.)

How Google+ Can Supercharge Your Beauty Salon Content Strategy

So far, Google+ has been sort of like that dog that keeps coming back into your yard searching for scraps. I mean, what should you do with him? The fact is, this dog can hunt! Beauty Salon businesses are starting to wake up to the opportunities with Google+, aiding not only with social media interaction, local visibility in the search engines, and helping to establish your beauty salon brand; but the numerous ways it helps you with content. And it's getting results: websites using the +1 Button increase page traffic by 350%, and more than 925,000 people join Google+ every day!

Seven Tips for Utilizing Your Google+ Page

Confused on how to use Google+? Don't worry – use these for starters!

1. **Your Google+ profile** – Complete it. Do this with a little

thought. Be sure you use engaging photos and images, and link to your other social media profiles.

2. **List your key information** – In particular hours of operation, contact details, along with maps and directions.

3. **Link to your sites** – make sure you link to your primary beauty salon business blog or site. This is a must!

4. **Create your beauty salon business page** –You can create content of any length, including video. This has strong benefits for search results as well as people who find you on Google+.

5. **Link out to your content** –Doing this will have several benefits, first of all getting them indexed almost instantly, along with a several other search engine advantages. You can also use your Google+ page to create posts, including multimedia which can link out to your content elsewhere.

6. **Utilize Direct Connect** – Utilize this feature in Google+ to allow visitors to add you to circles whenever they find you in search. Think of this as a Facebook "Like".

7. **Use video chat in Google+ Hangouts** – When you hold a video chat, Google+ streams it, records it, and supplies you with the recording via email. You may then upload to YouTube if you want, or use it on your website or in private. One fantastic option to use it is to create impromptu beauty salon product demos.

This is just the start of what's possible with Google+. To see even more methods plus a very cool infographic on the subject see this post on CopyBlogger.

5 Mobile Beauty Salon Marketing Strategies for a Shoestring Budget

Local mobile beauty salon marketing is a virtual goldmine!

However, given the marketing activities of most beauty salon businesses, you'd probably never know this.

The era of the smart phone is here but many local beauty salon business owners are still in the dark ages. They are playing catch up with their clients and their behavior. An interesting Web.com survey showed of 500 small business owners showed on 26 percent of respondents invested time and money in optimizing their site for mobile devices! What does this mean for beauty salon businesses? It means this is a great time to stand out from the crowd. The mobile customers are ripe for the taking and you are in perfect position to reap the rewards!

More than half of all searches are being done on a mobile device and you being a beauty salon business owner can take advantage of that. Even a beauty salon business on a tight budget can make use of these five ways to market to mobile beauty salon users.

- **Mobile Optimized Site** – Ensuring that the site is optimized properly for mobile is step one, and without it pretty much everything else doesn't matter. Make sure it is designed with mobile in mind, and is available on all platforms. According to market research from Google, 61 percent of consumers will leave a website if it's not optimized for mobile.

- **Look into Mobile Ads** – Mobile ads are cheap and efficient. This may sound surprising but right now a lot of the inventory goes unsold every month which keeps the costs down. This makes it a prime time for you to jump in and explore mobile advertising.

- **SMS and Push Notifications** – SMS messages (text messages) have a high open rate. According to Frost and Sullivan, they're opened at an amazing 95 percent! Push notifications are also an execllent way to stay in touch with your customers who choose to opt-in.

- **Combining Mobile and Your Social Media** – Nothing says social media like real-time connections with your customer base. This is the latest trend and the smallest of beauty salon businesses can get in on the craze by combining their social media site with a mobile devices. Combine specials, events, coupons or link a YouTube video to create buzz. Then Tweets and traffic will soon start coming to your web site. Next thing you know your site's search engine ranking will start climbing and so will your Google . However, the best part is, you'll be connecting with your subscriber base in a real-time way and they will give you valuable feedback.

嬾談 **Location Based Marketing and Passbook** – Be sure you're capable of being found with the various location based mobile services like Foursquare and Yelp, as well as look into new technology like Passbook, a terrific new app that enables users to store coupons, boarding passes, gift cards, event tickets, store cards, and other forms of mobile payment.

The most critical thing for local beauty salon businesses is to gather knowledge and always keep learning. Remember, it doesn't have to be difficult and it doesn't have to be expensive. You just have to begin where you are and never stop learning.

Beauty Salon Professionals: Facebook Is an Awesome Tool for Business, but Only When Wielded Awesomely

With nearly 10 billion users, Facebook is easily the most widely used social network in the world. If Facebook were a country with a seat at the U.N., it would have the third largest population, behind China and India. And like China and India, Facebook (should we call it Facebookistan?) features its own specific customs and norms, and you should understand and follow them so that you can capitalize on the site's potential as a tool for promoting and growing your business. When I see beauty salon businesses faceplant on Facebook, it's often because they don't invest some time to learn Facebookistan's customs.

Tread lightly

What makes Facebook different from other social networks? It's the fact that users have strong ties with each other. They are connected to their best friends, their family members, their in-laws as well as their long-lost friends from grade school. They share intimate areas of their lives.

Such things as:

> Birthday celebrations

> High school graduation footage

> Baby photos

> Wedding announcements

> Anniversaries

The upshot for beauty salon businesses? They need to be conscientious and careful within their technique. You can't use the old forms of one-way, direct-response marketing on Facebook, since people aren't there to listen to sales pitches. They're not in a buying mindset. They're in a socializing mindset. You should respect that.

Keep it real (for real)

If you are trying to port the old model of marketing into Facebook, you will be disappointed. "With Facebook, beauty salon business owners of any size can do effective, word-of-mouth marketing at scale for the very first time," says Annie Ta, a Facebook spokesperson. "But Facebook is all about authenticity, so if your beauty salon business is not being authentic or engaging with users in a way that feels genuine, the community will see through it."

If you're doing it right, it's hard

Don't be fooled by social media "gurus" who make wild promises about effortless Facebook success. Social media is all about building relationships and influence—and this needs time to work. Many organizations are under the impression that if they set up a page on Facebook, that's all they need to do. Marketing on Facebook is an incredibly effective way to reach local beauty salon clients and customers (we wouldn't be talking about it if it weren't). But here's the rub: it's also demanding (and rewarding) if you're doing it correctly. The payback is definitely worth the investment in time and attention. According to a study from Social Media Examiner, nearly two-thirds of small businesses engaged in social media state that Facebook has enhanced their overall marketing success, and 80 percent report forming new partnerships after just two years of participation.

Beauty Salon Business Owners: LinkedIn Is an Underrated Powerhouse, You're Crazy Not to Use It

LinkedIn is the Rodney Dangerfield of social media: despite having 200 million highly influential subscribers, it gets no respect. Even though it is consistently ranked among the social giants Facebook and Twitter, it doesn't seem to get as much hype from the mainstream media. But as a tool for marketing your beauty salon business, it provides a huge edge over its more popular peers. Because unlike Facebook and Twitter, which regularly exchange cat photos, inane one-liners and political rants from nutty uncles, LinkedIn is all business.

How companies are leveraging LinkedIn

You operate a beauty salon business. Your time and energy is scarce. So why should you worry about LinkedIn?

Here are a few ways your peers (there are 1.3 million small-business owners on the network) are employing it to their advantage:

- **Sharing wins**: As a beauty salon business owner, you're working hard. Why not share your success stories? Promoting your accomplishments is just good marketing. And with 2 million C-level executives using the site, you might suddenly find yourself with some deep-pocketed suitors.

- **Getting referrals**: LinkedIn makes it easy to get peer and client endorsements for the work you do. Best part? When someone recommends you or writes a testimonial, everyone within your network sees it in his or her activity feed. This type of social proof is the BEST way of getting new customers.

- **Finding new talent**: If your beauty salon business keeps growing, you'll undoubtedly need to hire new employees. LinkedIn is a great place—scratch that, it's the BEST place— to find new players to include in your team.

- **Promoting events**: LinkedIn's event feature is a game changer! It has never been so easy to spread the news and drum up enthusiasm about upcoming events, sales and get togethers. You can even use their service directory to find professional event planners to help you.

- 嫌談 **Boosting website traffic**: A little-known secret about LinkedIn is that it's very influential with Google; if you have a presence on LinkedIn, you're likely to see a jump in search engine visibility, too. More clicks = more customers!

- 鮎談 **Getting answers**: LinkedIn is a goldmine for information on operating a successful beauty salon business. You can uncover great advice from some of the savviest business minds in the world in LinkedIn Answers and Groups. You will discover over 2000 groups devoted to small-business and beauty salon business related topics.

- 承談 **Finding investors, vendors and partners**: It's a networker's paradise. Whether you require some capital, a new accounting firm, or even a beauty salon business partner, you're not going to find a better resource than LinkedIn. Anywhere.

We're just scratching the surface here, folks. The benefits don't end there. Pay a visit to LinkedIn, set up a page for your business and see for yourself. I know your time is scarce, but trust me, it's worth it.

Beauty Salon Professionals Are You Using Pinterest Yet? (You Should Be)

I know, I know. You don't have the time for an alternate social network. Nevertheless I wouldn't be doing my job if I didn't talk up Pinterest, as this image-centric social network has become an amazing spot for beauty salon businesses to:

- 〉 Meet new customers
- 〉 Boost website traffic
- 〉 Increase brand recognition
- 〉 Drive sales activity

So let's run through why this visual social network so cool—and so effective as a marketing strategy.

Visually pleasing! Less whining!

Instead of being a platform for tedious updates of what people ate for breakfast or ALL CAPS rants from your weird uncle, Pinterest is all about bringing people together who have common interests, whether it's fashion, beauty, art, food, crafts, architecture, photography, cocktail recipes, interior design..you name it. Copyblogger contributor Beth Hayden sums up Pinterest very well with this quote: "Pinterest is visually appealing, positive, and unlike Facebook, there isn't any whining." Can I get an amen?!

Why are marketers so energized about Pinterest?

For starters, the site is incredibly popular. Last year, in a five month span, Pinterest rocketed to a jaw-dropping 10 million users. No one was expecting it. Even social media watchers were caught off guard. Almost overnight Pinterest became a MAJOR driver of online traffic. Get this: Pinterest drives more traffic than YouTube, Google and LinkedIn—combined. Here's another thing: users love Pinterest. They can't get enough. It's addictive. As per comScore data Pinterest users average 89 minutes monthly on the site and Google users average just 3 minutes per month.

So what?

Why should beauty salon businesses like yours care about Pinterest? It's really quite simple. First of all, the site is a low-key, non-threatening method to meet consumers who are passionate about what you're interested in! This built-in permission makes it possible to build new relationships with others in your target market. Secondly, Pinterest is a fantastic place showcase your products or services, stay top of mind and grow your "tribe" of like-minded people. Just create an account. You'll see an array of businesses on the site, such as...

> Beauty Salon Businesses

> Hair Artists

> Makeup Artists

> Fitness Coaches

> Yoga Studios

> Non-profit Organizations

> Jewelry Makers

The list is endless.

No excuses; start pinning!

Most businesses tend to swiftly think of reasons why they shouldn't use social media—nevertheless the truth is, many sell themselves short and don't become involved because they don't think they have a natural place in a certain network. Now, if you run a bookkeeping business, maybe Pinterest isn't the best fit, but then again, it's quite possible that you might be a trailblazer and use Pinterest to showcase your business and have great success. Hey, if a plumbing franchise in Waco, Texas can make Pinterest benefit their business, you can too! It's just too easy to sell yourself short and come up with reasons to remain on the sidelines!

7 Simple And Fast Ways To Get More Beauty Salon Client and Customer Referrals

Everyone is always on the lookout for tips to get more beauty salon client referrals for their salon business. However, as stated by GrowThink.com some 58.6% of us don't even ask for them! Client and Customer referrals aren't something that appears just by wishing it so, but instead is a result of a clear, focused and consistently applied strategy. Listed below are seven ways we've found to increase client referrals, and they are surprisingly quicker and much easier than you might imagine!

1. **Recruit your best clients and customers** – Your best clients and customers might be your best option, as they are already in love with what you do don't need incentive to refer you to their circle of contacts. You just need to ask them!

2. **Offer incentives** – Special discounts, free things, upgrades or any other incentives appropriate for your business are a great way to get people to provide client and customer referrals.

3. **Go crazy on first-time clients and customers** – A new client and customer is a target ripe for the picking.

Make them feel so special and highly valued that they practically can't help telling everyone they know how good they were cared for.

4. **Engage your clients and customers** – Find creative ways to engage your clients and customers and possibly discover a way you can benefit each other. The secret is to get them talking, and being open to ideas. Create an online community for your clients and customers, say for example a blog or Facebook group.

5. **Be courteous and a giver** – Make saying "Thank You" part of your daily lexicon, and generous with regards to handing out perks. Laying an unexpected gift card or thank you note on a client or customer can be very beneficial.

6. **Enlist your staff** – Getting your employees in the game can boost your efforts. You will usually have to develop a way to reward results, but it can be very much worth the cost!

7. **Create a client or customer loyalty program** – A client or customer loyalty program, best administered online, is an awesome tool to help create interest and engagement.

A solid client and customer referral plan will take some effort, but can also produce a slew of new business pre-disposed to giving you a chance. What more can you ask?

5 CHAPTER
HOW TO USE YOUR HAIR ARTISTRY TO BUILD LOCAL AWARENESS AND MAKE A DIFFERENCE

Providing unique services that are elegant is a way forward for the success of your salon. Marketing is not all about communicating and persuading customers to buy your services or goods. The quality of the services you over is what matters. There is no need to market a service that is of poor quality since customers will try it and they will not come back for more. Your hair artistry is very important for local salon marketing.

Having unique hairstyles is the key point to the success of your salon. People love being unique in one way or another. Unique hairstyle is all they need to feel good and special. To focus on the different needs and desires of the clients, you must have different brands. Local salon branding will play a major role in attracting different clients with different needs. Not all hairstyle sell the same but it is good not to focus on one style that is selling most. If a client knows that he or she will get the wide range of hairstyles under one roof, they will remain loyal to you and they will keep coming for more services. Local salon business branding is not hard to implement.

All you need is the customer's interest at heart. A customer is perceived to be the king. You give him or her what they want to have. Customers are the one to help you in branding your business. Listen to what they say and do as they say. Listening to what customers say and acting fast on their needs will help your business grow faster and build a wide customer base. You will gain competitive advantage over other rivals and you will stand out as the best in the market. Having positioned your services in the mind of the customers, your hair artistry will make a difference.

People will be able to distinguish your services from those of other salons. Your local salon marketing campaigns will bear fruits as more people will come to your salon to experience the services the services you offer. When you offer a good service, the satisfied customers will talk good things about you and the word will spread like a fire. They will also feel free referring their friends and relatives to your business. The referral marketing and word of mouth is a viral marketing that requires no investment. The only thing required is providing good hair artistry that will appeal to many.

You have to put more efforts if you want to achieve in salon marketing. Your brands should stand out to be the best and unique. The uniqueness should be the selling point of your business and therefore you should concentrate more on your hair artistry. Give the best and the best will come back to you. Good marketing starts with the type of services you offer and the way you offer them. Be a professional when it comes to handling diverse customers with different taste and preference. That way you will build a strong relationship with your customers and your salon business will benefit.

Some people set goals to reflect only their salon business interests; others set only personal lifestyle goals. Once you get comfortable setting and reaching goals in one area, however, you may want to seriously think about setting and reaching goals in all areas of your life such as giving back to others. One of the ways I give back is through educational radio shows, seminars, donating my time and money to various beauty industry organizations and charities. The following are some ideas for you to create your salon business and lifestyle goals:

Personal Lifestyle Goals

There are a variety of goals that can come under the heading of personal lifestyle goals. You can break this category down much further into areas of your personal lifestyle that you would like to improve. For example, you may set relationship goals, self-improvement goals, personal issues that relate to your body, such as weight-loss or fitness goals, or even personal health goals.

Salon Professional Goals

This is one area where most people are comfortable setting goals. Salon professional goals usually have something to do with improving an area of your salon work life, such as preparing yourself to qualify for a certain salon job or improving on an area in your current salon job. Salon professional goals may also relate to getting the required education to qualify for a better salon job, or perhaps learning a new skill to start

your own salon business.

Perhaps you're terrified at starting your own business and need guidance. Maybe you already have the skills to start a salon business but you just can't bring yourself to do so. Moving past this obstacle could be a personal lifestyle goal or a salon professional goal; it doesn't really matter where you put it in your goal setting area. The only thing that matters is that you set the goal and begin to work on that area.

Financial Goals

Financial goals could be goals that mean you want to earn more money professionally or they could be goals where you work on spending less money in your personal life. Whatever area of your life is affected, that is where you want to put your financial goals. Whether it is a personal lifestyle goal or a salon professional goal isn't what's important. What is important is that you identify an area of your life where you are committed to making an improvement and begin by writing down your goal setting strategy.

A Goal for Each Area of Your Life

Balance is the key when it comes to setting and reaching goals. That's because setting and reaching goals is a tool we use to lead happy and successful lives. For this reason, try not to have every goal in one category only, such as your salon professional goals or your financial goals. In fact, see how many categories you can think of to set goals in order to help you achieve that balance. Did you know that some people even need to set goals for their leisure life? That's right! See how many categories you can come up with to set and reach goals. Go ahead, have fun; don't limit goals to the work part of life; set goals for fun too!

6 CHAPTER

HOW TO CREATE A SIX FIGURE INCOME USING YOUR POWERFUL HAIR ARTISTRY SKILLS

If you have always had interest in the beauty business and wanted to earn a six figure income as a hairstylist. It is advisable to put into consideration the idea of becoming a hairstylist with multiple skills such as makeup artistry and skin care. With cosmetics being the largest segment of the beauty industry, you would have a greater chance getting to six figures honing your makeup skills. It would really benefit you most getting connected with the top celebrity beauty professionals in the industry and learning as much as you can.

Being a professional makeup and hair artist allows you to play a very crucial role in some of the events which are very remarkable such as weddings as well as other events which are personal, award presentations that are televised, in movies or any other crucial events where there is a necessity of the makeup artist or hairstylists' services.

Makeup artistry and hair artistry career involves offering personal appearance or beauty services which improves the consumer's look. These services majorly include makeovers, cutting, shampooing, hair styling as well as hair coloring. They can also provide advisory services to the clients on how they can easily manage and take care of their skin or hair as well as on what they should do so as to improve their hair or skin condition. To add on that, the hairstylist can also give pointers on how to make use of the makeup that looks best with their hairstyle as well as the shape of their face.

As a freelance artist, personal appearance is very important. Freelance specialists who can give offer various services are more preferred than those who lack the ability to perform. This means in order to be successful in the freelancing career you must undergo continued training. Some ongoing skills training maybe learning to do pedicures, manicures, face and scalp treatment, provide the analysis of makeup as well as being able to clean and also style hair extensions and wigs.

Apart from having the opportunity to make interaction with many celebrities, you will also enjoy a schedule that is very flexible which will allow you time for family at home and leisure activities. You will also have the pleasure of being your own boss hence working under no pressure from anyone.

Furthermore, there is an added advantage of receiving invitation to parties, openings of clubs, galas as well as many concerts. This will also lengthen your list engagements which are social in your work of hairstylist. You may get special satisfaction in working with special populations that include catering to disabled and cancer survivors which I am very passionate about.

To be a successful hairstylist, you will need to become certified. All countries and states require cosmetologists, barbers, hairstylists as well as the makeup artist to be fully licensed; only the shampooers are exempted. Even though there is the variation of the hairstylist requirement condition from state to state, the required minimum age remain constant.

There are great opportunities in the beauty field only if you are well trained as a hairstylist and licensed as well as when able to offer variety of services to clients. The measure of the advantage you get will be the steady build up and increase of your clientele since you are doing the job for yourself.

In the beginning, it's fun to write your hairstylist business goals down, especially if you have a fancy new notebook or you have constructed a special program or spreadsheet to use in your computer. What gets old is keeping up with the hairstylist business goals once you've set them. In the following paragraphs, we'll look at three simple steps you can use to get and stay motivated to set and reach your hairstylist business goals.

1. **Visualization**

It's easy enough to talk about visualization – the act of visualizing your hairstylist business goal already accomplished – but how often do you let yourself get carried away. This is exactly what successful people do. Are you implementing this?

2. **Notation**

How many times do you revisit your hairstylist business goals you write down and update your progress? How many steps have you been able to cross off your list? Remember, hairstylist business goals are simply specific steps that are broken down into manageable pieces. For example, if your hairstylist business goal is to have ten brand new clients in a certain amount of time, when you have gained only two, don't moan and groan that you have gained only two clients; instead divide those ten clients into increments of two clients each and go in to your hairstylist business goal setting list and cross those two clients off. Now rewrite your hairstylist business goals to gain eight new clients. Don't you feel a sense of accomplishment? Of course you do! You see, small steps like these are what reaching hairstylist business goals of any size are all about.

3. Celebration

You don't have to wait until your hairstylist business goal is 100% completely reached to celebrate. Celebrate each step of the hairstylist business goal reaching ladder if you like. Do whatever it takes to stay motivated. For example, if your hairstylist business goal is to save $1,000 for a special hairstylist retreat event, don't be discouraged when you realize part way through your hairstylist business goal timetable that you only have $350 saved. Celebrate! Buy yourself a hairstylist retreat magazine that features your destination or if you don't want to spend any money at all, work in to your food budget a special dish from the area of your planned vacation. Spend the evening cooking a themed dinner and listening to the kind of music you'll hear on your special retreat. Celebrate each step of the hairstylist business goal setting and reaching process until you're all the way there!

When you are inclined in the profession of hair styling, perhaps one of your greatest dreams is to be part of the few yet very good top hair dressers in your country or even in the world. It's a very difficult journey but not an impossible one. It is not even impossible for those who have no knowledge and zero training at all, for the most important factor to be successful in this field is your determination, commitment, and your very own unique eyes. If it's possible to be the industry's leader, where should you start?

1. **Start by acquainting yourself with the numerous hair cutting and styling methods and techniques**. This would eventually consume

bulk of your time. Even when you already consider yourself as a professional, there are still some items to consider and lessons to learn. An aspiring top hair stylist will not progress when there are gaps and omissions in his or her learning curve. Neither can he or she keep up with competition if he or she is unaware of cuts and styles others are offering.

2. **Start with a few yet loyal clienteles**. Though you would want to be recognized by as many people as possible to be the best hair stylist, it still pays to be patient and let the laws of nature and economics take their course. Concentrate on giving your best shot even with a few clients that you currently have, for the good news (your very good work) will eventually spread out. Instead of allotting your time massively promoting your services elsewhere, just prepare for the load of referrals that your current customers may provide when you get your job done exceptionally.

3. **The industry leaders have keen pair of eyes capable of identifying hair styles whether they look good or exceptionally good**. They are concentrated on providing the latter. Getting a haircut and hair styling done good means that your work is merely acceptable and is common. Creating an exceptional look suggests that your work is hailed above the average and an exception to what is acceptable, that it is somewhat unique and can only be tagged as your own creation.

4. **Bring your imaginations to life**. Most of the time, the best hair stylist can already imagine the perfect cut, twists, and curls at the mere instant of seeing the client's hair. It's a very good sign of an artistic and skillful mind. Implement all your planned creations however odd-looking they may be. The top hair stylists of today made their mark with the help of their crazy ideas.

5. **Search for a good mentor**. Aside from the lessons which may be imparted to you, explore more for other ideas. Join seminars and conventions on hair styling. When given an opportunity, seek employment under one of the best hair and fashion stylist in your country or area, even just as an assistant. You will eventually learn some tips and tricks by mere watching and listening.

6. **Establish communication or a strong relationship with each of your client**. If possible, get to know their personalities and lifestyles.

It's not only a form of excellent customer service but also a chance for you to learn even more.

Starting a salon business can be tough. Maintaining one is relatively easy when you understand how to attract salon business. Attracting clients to your salon is more or less an art that all salon owners need to perfect in order to ensure a long lasting business relationship with your clients and by extension, your business.

Location

When starting a salon business, understand that you will need to market your services aggressively so as to get the word out. Ensure that your salon is located at an easy to reach area that does not look neglected or surrounded by other businesses that will make customers shy away. For example, do not locate a business near an area with a shabby looking club.

Appeal and Salon Beauty

Ensure you have the right appeal. This means that you should have a well-designed and organized space. This will reduce accidents and ensure smooth movement in and out of you salon. Well-designed posters that advertise your space will attract all the salon business clients walking by your salon. When renovating the space, use more glass fronts to show the world that this is indeed a salon.

Advertise

Many attracting salons ignore the idea of advertising and just rely on word of mouth. Although word of mouth is in itself an advertising strategy, it is rarely enough. Take advantage of social sites and open up a space for your business online. If possible, start a website that talks about your salon.

More aggressively, place ads on well-known salon blogs and sites and on the social sites as well. In case you already have a website, link it with social sites so that you increase traffic to your sites. Take advantage of search engines and advertise on their first page with key words such as salon and hair care.

Posters

Another salon client attraction is to place posters on notice boards of nearby schools and campuses near your salon. Students love to keep their hair looking good and they will serve as a great advertising channel. Ensure that your posters are appealing to the eye. Don't just type something and stamp it on the notice board. Go the extra mile, print something good and you are on your way to attracting all the salon business clients you need.

Customer Satisfaction

Keep your customers happy. Do not tell them how to style their hair. Give them the first chance to speak and let you know what they want. Do not try to be a know it all and force a client to pick a certain style. Be direct and honest too. If you do not know how to do a certain style being requested by the client, say so. Many salon workers listen to the client just to provide an answer. Listen to understand the client first then you give her or him your piece of mind. This will win so many clients and they will come asking for you every time as they want to be attended to by the person who gets them. These tips will help you to attract salon clients and to keep your salon business running.

7 CHAPTER
HOW TO CREATE A PROFITABLE SALON BUSINESS WITHOUT DRAINING YOUR BANK ACCOUNT

With changing times, the demand for beauty business is on a rise. People today are keener on investing in their personal beauty regimens. That's primarily because many have understood the importance of creating the perfect first impression that will help them win business contracts, promotions, great deals and even love. This increasing inclination of people towards enhancing their appearance has helped many creative professionals like make-up artists, hair artists and hairstylists to improve their earnings. Many experienced and talented beauty industry professionals even consider starting their own beauty salon business.

Starting your own beauty salon business might seem very overwhelming particularly if you are someone who is starting from scratch and has no idea about managing your own beauty salon business. To begin with, planning is the basic activity that you will need to do to start your own beauty salon. Like any other beauty salon business, only the right plan will make you successful. When you are planning to set up your own beauty salon, you must consider the location, the kind of beauty salon you want to have, the services you want to offer, your budget, etc. These basic details are very important to make sure you set your business up for success.

Experience is another important skill that you need for starting out on your own. You might be a trained hairstylist, hair artist or makeup artist holding a professional degree from a reputed hair and beauty institute. However, that will not guarantee you all the success. People who come to you want to be sure that you have the right experience to give them the perfect hair or beauty makeover. This is perhaps the reason why it is recommended that you gain some experience by working in a beauty salon before starting your own beauty salon. This will also help you with your ground work on how things work. Working at a successful beauty salon will give you practical training on how a successful beauty salon should operate.

It is absolutely important to have a budget in mind. As a matter of fact, there is no perfect plan without budget. When you have your finances clearly defined, you can take the right steps towards success. Without having the budget laid out, there are good chances that you may end up purchasing for your beauty salon things that you don't need. You will have to invest in the right kind of furniture and tools for your beauty salon. While selecting the furniture, you need to precisely select that which is comfortable for your customers.

Lastly, when establishing your own beauty salon; you need to bear in mind that establishing a good customer base is more important. Marketing your services is important to let people know that your beauty salon exists. Your marketing efforts should also include building rapport and connection with your present customers. Only when you are able to retain your customers while making strategies to increase your customer base, will you be able to establish your new beauty salon as a successful venture.

In today's competitive and constantly changing salon business environment it can be a challenge for a salon business to be successful. In order to be a successful salon business you must make salon goals and plan to achieve them. There are three essential areas of good salon business goal planning that will help you achieve your salon business goal. They are: strategies, skills and systems.

Salon Business Strategies

A strategy is the development and execution of a plan directed toward a specified business goal. You must have a defined salon business goal to employ a strategy. It is also important to select the right salon business strategy.

Salon Business Skills

Salon Business skills play a vital role in the development of your salon business. The more skills you have the more confidence you will have in directing your efforts toward a desired salon business goal. Salon Business management and self-management skills are the two most important sets of salon business skills that an effective salon business owner will develop.

Planning involves the ability to prioritize activities in your personal life and the workload in your salon business life. This means determining what things need to be done first and doing those things before the interruption of other things. Many unsuccessful salon business people fail because they become overwhelmed. Prioritizing and planning will eliminate the feeling of being overwhelmed.

The language we use to communicate with others is very important when we are running a salon business and our emotional state of mind can influence our language. However, aside from the emotional context, the language we use to direct and to serve people says volumes about our managing abilities. Positive language always achieves better results. You will find it much easier to be positive in your communication if you are certain about the salon business goals for which you are aiming.

You also need to be able to communicate your salon business goals to people within your organization. Of course there are other elements involved in effective marketing, but it all starts with effective communications. You need to make salon business goals about how you will manage people working for you too. This requires you to be able to train, evaluate and monitor the progress of those people who are working for you. It also means having the ability to direct and delegate responsibilities to achieve the most effective results for your salon business.

Salon Business Systems

All successful salon businesses have systems in place that help that salon business grow. Systems allow salon owners to monitor salon business performance and modify it as the profit margin dictates. Salon business systems also help maintain consistency in operations from management to salon sales. Salon business systems can, when properly utilized, have a positive impact on driving up your profits, but only if you have clear salon business goals with which to guide these salon business systems.

Unless you, as a salon business owner, plan the future of your salon business, you will not be able to rise above the cut throat competition. If you plan your salon business you will succeed in the salon business plan. You and your team will be clear about what needs to be achieved and what the agreed strategies are for achieving these salon business goals. This should allow you to pull together for maximum effectiveness and maximum profit.

Salon business goal setting is an important part of planning your salon business and establishing yourself as a credible salon business. By setting challenging salon business goals, you will find that you are motivated to assertively push your salon business forward and gain many benefits by accomplishing your mission.

It all starts with understanding what goal setting is all about. Goal setting is the process of creating a plan that is comprised of multiple steps to reach a specific result.

1. The first step is defining the salon business goal you want to accomplish. For example, I want to create a salon business that produces X products for sale and attracts Y number of clients and customers monthly.

2. The second step is to create milestones or multiple steps to accomplish that salon business goal. For example, the first milestone may be to research and evaluate effective salon business product ideas. The next milestone may be to create a salon business website layout to reflect the salon business theme. Other milestones will help you achieve your ultimate salon business goal.

3. The third step is to create a process for managing and evaluating progress against milestones to reach your salon business goal. Setting timelines for your milestones will help. For example, conduct and complete salon business product research by Dec 15 may be a milestone. Evaluating your progress will include confirming that you have met your Dec 15th deadline for completing this work. If you have missed your deadline, you will know that you must be more attentive and aggressive to accomplish your milestones.

With salon business goal setting, keep in mind that you will always have "short term salon business plans" to reach "long-term salon business goals". This means that interim steps along the way are important to your success for the future. Salon business goal setting is like having a roadmap to your destination.

Think about taking a trip to a beauty retreat for a week. If you simply get in your car on Friday and start driving with no clear direction on which highway to take, which direction to drive (Pacific or Atlantic ocean?), and how to get to your beauty retreat location, you will have difficulty or may never reach your beauty retreat goal. If you do reach your beauty retreat destination, you may find that your retreat reservation was for Saturday but you arrived on Friday!

However, if you have a clear goal in mind to arrive at the beauty retreat on Saturday, December 15 and stay at the Holiday Inn and Suites, then you can create milestones to reach your goal. You decide whether to drive or fly, purchase an airline ticket if necessary, plan the day you will leave, what to pack, make a beauty retreat reservation, and everything else in between. Your goal of having a fun-filled week at the retreat in December becomes a reality with proper planning!

Your salon business works the same way. Establishing your salon business goal, creating milestones, and measuring progress will help you succeed. You may find that you need to adjust plans along the way to accomplish your salon business goal or you may decide to refine your salon business goals. But the most important thing is that you have a salon business goal and plan.

When it comes to setting your salon business goals, remember:

1. Establish a long-term salon business goal.

2. Create interim salon business milestones that have dates for accomplishment.

3. Measure progress against salon business milestones, keeping the ultimate goal in mind at all times.

4. Make adjustments in salon business milestones as needed to succeed.

Proper salon business goal setting and management is the road to salon business success when it comes to creating, managing, and maintaining your salon business.

And remember, "plan your work, and work your plan"!

Salon Business Goal Setting Worksheet

Salon business goal setting worksheets can be an integral component of your salon business goal setting strategy. With the proper salon business planning and creation of salon business goals, milestones, and methods of evaluation, your dreams will become a reality much quicker and with greater success. A salon business goal setting worksheet can be an incredible asset in this process, saving you time, money, and effort. Salon business goal setting worksheets are a compilation of all of the actions required to reach a desired result.

Take a look at the salon business goal setting worksheet process to help you with your salon professional goal setting process. Salon business goal setting worksheets include the milestones to help you accomplish your ultimate salon business goals. Many people refer to salon business goal setting worksheets as 'salon business action plans' since they are filled with actions to be taken towards the accomplishment of a salon business goal. The milestones are considered "salon business short term goals" and they are essential to reaching your long-term ultimate goal towards salon business success.

Setting up a good salon can be a hard task as it requires huge capital for premises, buying machines, equipment, hiring expert employees and buying different beauty products that will be used by different clients in the salon. In order to have a good salon, it highly recommended that a starter writes a good salon business plan to act as a guide. The plan can be bought from an expert business writer. In addition to a good plan, a well-structured salon marketing plan should also be considered to boost the brand and the new image.

Starting your salon business

There are many problems encountered when in the process of a salon business start-up. This can be solved through the procedure below.

First one should get licenses from relevant authorities. A cosmetology license should also be acquired. After the licenses, decide on how to fund the start-up capital. This can be from loans, savings or business partnerships. Salon business plan will be required when seeking out loans.

Look for a unique location in your area. A clean and spacious area is ideal and it should be near a shopping center to get more clients. A business checking account should be opened so that expenses will be easier to pay and even get the business deposits. Getting insurance will also be factored here.

Get the best salon equipment that are in the market today. Make the interview for salon assistants to help in running the business. After all has been set, it is recommended that one gets a day for grand opening. This day can be used to offer less costly services to clients so that they know the business existences.

How to market your salon

It is important for new salon business owners to engage in salon marketing as this will define the success. Here are some simple ways to market the business.

First it is important to train the employees on the best ways to treat the clients. In this they should ensure they retain the clients through good customer relations.

It will be a good idea to talk to other businesses around. Use some flyers in their business so that they can be given to customers when they visit. Posters are also a good way to market the salon. This should contain good information on service offered.

Set aside some resources to put adverts on local magazines, books and coupons. This is less costly but reaches many potential clients. In addition the local radio and television channels can be approached for advertising spaces. There are some stations that will give the salon business out of pockets services by donating some products to the company to be sold at half prices. This will attract many people to your salon business.

Getting a website or domain name is an important tool used in salon marketing. The website should contain all the necessary information that clients will be looking for. The site should be simple to use, easy to navigate and contain pictures and videos that are attractive. Good design of the website should be factored.

8 CHAPTER
HOW TO CREATE SYSTEMS THAT WORK FOR YOU AND YOUR TEAM

The beauty business is one of the most noble of callings, despite the vanity it invokes. The ability to boost confidence and enhance appearance is highly regarded, highlighting the importance of salons and boutiques. These are also businesses like any other, and measures must be put in place to improve production and sustain profits at an optimum.

A salon is a customer centric business. This implies that the customer indeed is king, and maintaining a close relationship with them is necessary. Client gathering, impeccable service and follow up are important to foster loyalty. This will go a long way in guaranteeing a steady flow of business regardless of the season.

Client gathering

Adverts on the style section of the local newspaper are bound to arouse attention to the business. Have a phone line on the ready, with a friendly attendant to answer any calls and queries. More so, advertising during special events such as weddings and fashion shows is a successful first attempt at getting new clients.

In addition, have former clients inform their friends and family on the experience they had. If the service and styling was excellent, rest assured that a steady stream of new customers will be generated. Motivate current clients to market the business to others via discounts and loyalty programs. This is a very effective salon marketing system.

Client follow-up

Every client-centered business requires that the customer be kept "warm". A salon follow-up system is integral in sustaining a personalized relationship with the client. It may be done in various ways, such as call-ups to confirm appointments.

Calls and emails inquiring about the experience will also go a long way towards establishing a friendly rapport with clients. Amicable beauticians will make the client happy to make subsequent appointments. They are also highly likely to tag their friends along.

Team management

The salon staff ought to be familiar with their trade. They must also be aware of the concept of customer satisfaction, and be ready to establish a working relationship with valuable clients.

Salon team management is a very important concept. Care should be taken to ensure none of the attendants is idle at any time. Work plans that are in line with the appointments should be put in place. Ensure that the staff is always highly motivated for the best results.

Salon accounting systems

A salon business is an enterprise like any other, and with this in mind, there must be means of measuring revenues and costs. This means that accounting systems must be set up and implemented successfully to provide the metrics of success, or unlikely failure of the salon business.

Inventory management, accounting for successful sales and expenses incurred are some of the means to measure productivity. Profits, cash flow and losses are elementary concepts that are influential in the business. These will make processes such as seeking financial assistance and tax compliance and reporting very easy.

A successful salon business requires dedication and business acumen, just like any enterprise. An understanding of its nature is a vital requirement: from the client acquisition to the accounting methods and team management.

It is the dream of every salon owner or manager to have the business grow. For this to happen the salon must have a good working team that is able to gain the loyalty of clients and thus retain old clients and at the same time attract new clients. To have a good salon team a salon owner or manager should not just think of how to motivate the team, but on how to create a good working environment where the salon team can motivate themselves.

Great talent will always prefer to work in a salon where they are highly valued and motivated. Money can be earned anywhere therefore as a good salon leader it is your duty to keep a good working team and at the same time attract new good talent. Nowadays people don't just looking for a job, they look for a good opportunity to grow professionally.

When you want to hire a new salon team member the most valued qualities one should consider include: politeness, enthusiasm, proactive and a person with a good image and can smile to clients. Smiling is a valued trait in any salon business. A person who is smiling cannot be angry at the same time. Thus when clients come to positive and smiling environment they are motivated to come back again and this will contribute to the growth of the salon as a whole.

The following should be considered when looking for a potential salon team member:

1. Is the person happy with the salon environment? Is he or she smiling?

2. Does the person have a commitment to personal success?

3. Is the person well-dressed? They should be smartly dressed to create a good image for the business.

4. Are they conversant with the latest styles and trends that are featured on magazines and runways?

5. Is the person ready to make some sacrifices for the general success of the salon?

6. Did the person arrive on time for his or her interview?

Incentives generally play a major role in attracting and retaining a good working salon team.

The following are some of the cost effective incentives that can help motivate the salon team:

1. **Develop a culture of rewarding the person who sells most salon services and retail products every month**. Rewards can be as simple as allowing her or him a free hair make-up that month or an opportunity to attend a career show.

2. **Offer to pay a certain percentage of money for a relevant training course in order to encourage every staff to continuously acquire new skills**. This will not only keep each member of staff motivated to work but will created a justifiable platform to adequately charge for the services that you offer.

3. **Encourage your team members to participate in trade competitions.** This will help them increase their skills and confidence at work.

4. **Invite producers and manufacturers to carry out training sessions at you salon**. This will give every staff member an opportunity to attend and learn new skills.

5. **Support spirit and motivation days**. At least once a month sponsor a day where every team members gets a chance to have his or her nails, hair and waxing done at the expense of the salon. This will ensure every team members looks smart and this will help you keep your salon team.

As a good salon owner or manager make it a personally responsibility to create favorable working conditions for your staff because it is only then that the business is assured of success.

Now that you are involved with salon business sales as your career, you will no doubt have a quota that your salon employer wants you to hit. This is your salon sales goal and at least part of your salary may be dependent upon achieving that salon sales goal. That can be a good incentive but it can also be a worry!

Sometimes we set our own salon sales goals and sometimes the company sets them for us. But whichever, if we are serious about our salon sales goal setting, we need to make a practical plan in some detail which shows how we will achieve these salon sales goals. So few salon managers and hairstylists actually think to do that. No wonder so few salon sales goals are met!

So let's have a look at how you can have more success at meeting your salon sales goals. First, you have to plan effectively. Your salon sales should be SMART – specific, measurable, achievable, realistic and timed. Failure to make a detailed plan that starts with these basics accounts for almost all failures to achieve salon sales goals.

Once you have SMART targets, you can start to break the salon sales goal down into smaller, bite-size objectives. That way, you can see what you need to do on a weekly or daily basis in order to achieve your salon sales goals.

So how do you start with this kind of salon sales goal setting?

First, ensure that you have a definite and clear objective. You may want to achieve, for example, $1,000 in new salon clients this year and $1,000 from repeat salon clients in a year. Once you have this goal in mind, you should break these salon sales goals down into what you need to achieve each month or each week. Count on closing only approximately a third of the potential clients you get. That would be about the average. Bear that in mind when you are working what you need to do short-term in order to set you on the path toward that annual salon sales goal.

You should find that suddenly your annual salon sales goals are not so frightening and are actually quite achievable. If they don't seem realistic and achievable to you, you may have to modify your annual salon sales goals.

Once you know you have the right salon sales goals, it's time to set about trying to achieve them. Make yourself daily objectives. Half the difficulty in achieving salon sales goals is in getting started, so once you have started, you're on your way. Start today!

You should keep track of everything you do toward achieving your salon sales goals. Track all your salon meetings, and what salon sales you close on. That way, you can measure your success and modify your efforts as you need to. This measurement should soon suggest to ways in which you could improve your salon sales performance. You should take responsibility for these things that you need to change – and change them!

Set specific time aside each week or each when you will implement the specific actions you planned toward your salon sales goals. You can't expect to improve your sales if you don't put in the time and effort. Keep this implementation time sacred. Don't get distracted by emails or phone calls; just do what you planned to do.

You always need to reinforce your salon sales goals, in order to keep your motivation going. Chart your progress toward your salon sales goals on a regular basis and take the time to notice and be proud of your achievements. Realize how this progress makes further salon sales goals possible, so re-assess your salon sales goals regularly too, so you achieve as much as you can and feel a sense of achievement along the way.

9 CHAPTER
HOW TO INCREASE YOUR RETAIL SALES AND REVENUE GROWTH

Hair salons are a super competitive business to be involved. There are many ways to gain an edge over the competition and grow sales. The main ways to increase sales in the door are to get more customers, offer more services or products, and to charge more for services. The simplest method of increasing revenues is to get more clients. There are many methods of advertising to get more people in the door.

The most effective advertising with salons is word of mouth. Offer high quality work and exceptional customer service and current clients will rave about how great your salon is. In order to enlarge your client list quicker you may also want to advertise in a local magazine or paper that targets your preferred clients, put an ad on a billboard or for more modest budgets put posters at trendy bars or coffee shops or pass out coupons.

People are willing to try out a new business if the deal is good enough so a coupon giving away your services lower for the first visit will get customers in the door, after that it's up to you to provide the service, value and atmosphere that will make them want to pay full price on their next visit.

The most dramatic way to increase revenue is to offer more services and products. Begin offering beauty treatments that your salon does not currently offer. Offering high end beauty treatments will increase revenues gradually as a higher end clientele begins coming to your salon. A quicker increase will be seen by offering celebrity style services such as make over sessions, girls night outs and other pamper me sessions.

A more subtle approach to offering more products is to keep both lower and higher end hair and beauty supplies for sale. Most people will see the price of the lower end supplies and decide to buy something and at the point where they have decided to buy it's very easy to up sell them the higher end supplies. No one wants to take a chance with their appearance when for just a little bit more they can get the top of the line products.

Charging more for your services is the trickiest of all the ways to increase revenue. You have to be able to offer services above and beyond what the competition is offering. If all your clients are leaving your salon feeling and looking like a million dollars then you may be able to charge a premium for your exceptional services. The downside is that this may also scare away some customers. If a niche can be found for this business then it will be extremely profitable. But in most cases you are better off offering exceptional services for competitive prices.

Quality is the key to each of the methods listed. If your salon doesn't offer services that make people want to come back then that's a customer lost. Every regular client that you hold increases revenues as often as that person comes in, whether it is monthly, weekly, or annually. With such a competitive industry every dollar and every customer counts, don't waste an opportunity to increase your client list.

Creating your short and long-term hairstylist business goals will provide you with a roadmap to success. Keep these tips in mind when creating your hairstylist business goals.

1. **Visualize your hairstylist business goals and success** – plant it firmly in your mind as you begin creation of the actions required.

2. **Evaluate and consider your resources, skills, and abilities**. Determine where there may be a lack of ability or skills and determine how to compensate for this deficit.

3. **Make sure the actions are clear and concise**. Break them down into smaller steps for greater success.

4. **Use positive words in your actions and steps**. Positive-thinking has a powerful impact on our ability to succeed. A "self-fulfilling" prophecy, which means we become what we think we can become, is important to remember when creating a hairstylist business goal setting worksheet.

5. **Use affirmative words in action plans**. Don't say "I think I will complete the research by Dec 15", or "I want to.....". Instead, use affirmative statements such as "Complete the

market research on potential niche products by Dec 15."

6. **Create relevant actions that will help you achieve your hairstylist business goals**.

7. **Monitor your actions and deliverables frequently**.

8. **Create ticklers or calendar alerts to remind you of pending due dates**. Don't wait until the action is due to evaluate progress.

9. **Set reminders on your calendar or email to remind you to accomplish certain actions or steps along the way**. It's impossible to keep track of everything in your head and this can sabotage your efforts if you don't have an organized plan to manage actions towards hairstylist business goals.

10. **Plan the necessary steps towards your ultimate hairstylist business goals and monitor them frequently**!

Creating a hairstylist business goal setting worksheet is a tremendous asset to you in your salon professional goal setting strategy and creating your hairstylist career. It gives you the tools, steps, and actions needed to succeed. Once you have a clearly defined hairstylist business goal setting worksheet with achievable, challenging action steps, you'll be on your way to hairstylist success! It's the blueprint to increasing your retail sales and revenue growth.

10 CHAPTER
HOW TO INCREASE YOUR CLIENT AND CUSTOMER REFERRALS

Hairstyling has become one of the most demanded services under beauty care and personal grooming. With more and more people showing enthusiasm in experimenting with their looks, the need for professional hairstylists has increased extensively. Many people interested in the fashion industry have taken up hairstyling professionally to help people enhance the way they look. If you are someone who is interested in the hair business, you will need to join a good cosmetology school to get the best hair stylist degree. Once you become an expert at hair cutting, weaving, coloring and styling hair in the best way possible. There is a lot more that you need to learn once you graduate if you want to run your hair salon business effectively.

Like any other industry, the beauty and grooming industry has quite a lot of competition. This means that to survive in this industry, you will need to use your expertise to build your credibility and attract customers to your salon. When it comes to your hair business, it is only a good clientele base that will help you own a successful salon business. A good marketing strategy is one of the most important keys to becoming a successful hairstylist. During bad economic times people would still visit a hair salon in order to look good and feel better.

Increasing your client base or keeping your client loyal to you might seem overwhelming. However, if you have an effective marketing plan, this is not really difficult to accomplish. Here are some basic marketing ideas that you can use to increase your customer base:

- The best way to build your customer base is to keep in constant contact with your customers. As a matter of fact, it is recommended that you create a beauty club where you enroll members. You may want to offer special deals and offers to the members of your club. This will ensure that you have a loyal client base.

- When you begin your hair salon business, you can even send a flyer to everyone you know to make them aware of your hair styling business. You can even offer a free first appointment or any special deal to invite more customers.

- With hair salon businesses, it is extremely important to build a good rapport with your clients to keep them coming back to you. You can maintain a database of your clients with the birthday, anniversary, etc to call them on these special occasions and offer them a discount. You can even have festival offers to attract new customers.

While it is true that your hair salon business will grow by word of mouth, you cannot solely depend on this source to stay in business. Planning your marketing strategy is essential to have a successful hair salon business.

Marketing your salon is very important for the growth your business. Customers need to know the presence of your salon and the services you offer. People cannot know your business and the services you offer unless you communicate to them.

That communication is what is referred to as marketing. The more brilliant way of marketing your salon is by providing excellent services. Customers want to be treated like kings and queens. If you treat them the way they want, you will see them again coming for more services. Satisfied customers will talk good things about your business and are likely to refer more people to your salon. You will be able to build a link of loyal customers and your business will grow in a fast way.

Providing good services alone is not enough for marketing your business. There are other ways you can use to market your salon and attract more clients. Here are some of the best ways you can use to market your salon.

1. **Create a logo for your salon**. Having and nice logo and style for your business is very important in positioning you brand in the mind of the customers. Design a logo that will portray well the image of your business. Let the professionalism of the services you offer be seen through the logo and the style.

2. **Create a marketing slogan**. Create a slogan that will set you apart from other competitors. It is not necessarily for outside

marketing but also for internal purposes. Let it focus on the strong attributes of your salon that other salons don't have.

3. **Put up an appealing signage**. Install and attractive signage around your business and the surroundings. Make it more attractive and to reflect the core values of your business. If it is not enough to put the signage around your business, you can place more at the surrounding of your business.

4. **Create and promote a website for your salon**. Design a good website that will enable you sell the services your offer to clients. Most people are searching for products and services online therefore, if your business will target such customers, you will create a huge customer base which is more beneficial. Optimize your web page to appear in the front page of the search engines.

5. **Market your salon through email marketing**. Email marketing will keep you in touch with your customers. Collect emails from your customers and potential customers. Send them updates about the new services you offer and the improvement or changes you have made. Customers will feel more valued if you stay close to them.

6. **Advertise your salon through regular advertising such as billboards, newspapers, posters, television and radios**. You will be able to reach a wider audience of potential customers.

Choose this type of marketing depending on the size of your salon and the target market.

In conclusion, marketing your salon is a brilliant idea that will make your business grow and become appealing. Good marketing will enable you position your services in the mind of the customers. If you position your business correctly and always stay in the mind of the customers, then you will be successful.

11 CHAPTER
HOW TO INCREASE YOUR VISIBILITY IN THE MARKETPLACE

The visibility of your salon in the beauty market place matters a lot in the success of your business. Everything that you do including the services you offer should be aimed at increasing your salon visibility. Having a large customer base will increase salon profits. The major aim or goal of the business is to make profits and therefore you have to work hard to achieve it. Competition in the beauty market place is high; you need to make your salon stand out as the best in the beauty market.

There are ways you can implore to increase salon visibility. Some of them are very easy to perform. You need to recognize the community that is supporting your business by giving back to them. Public relation activities can increase salon credibility since people will feel attached to the salon and there is mutual benefit. Here are some of the public relation activities that will increase your salon visibility.

1. **Participating in cleaning the environment**. Provide dust bins for the surrounding community to help in collecting waste materials. Put some advertising massages on the dustbins and distribute them to every corner. This will help a lot in making the environment look clean. The community will appreciate the offer and they will be your loyal customers.

2. **Helping the needy**. There are other people who are less fortunate in the community around you. Donate food, time, clothes and sleeping materials. Do it for free and you will build a good public image that will reflect positively on the services you offer. Changing the lives of people is not very easy but if stay if you manage to transform them to a better level, they will never forget you. It will build a permanent relationship between your salon and the community.

3. **Support the bright students by giving school bursaries and sponsorship**. There are brighter students in the community surrounding you that needs help in their education. Help

such students by sponsoring their education and offering them job opportunities once they have completed their studies. Employing people you have assisted to shape their lives will increase employee loyalty and they will work hard to make your services better. Some of them are more talented and they will come up with new ideas that will help you expand your business. your business will grow rapidly in the right way.

4. **Provide employment opportunities**. In order to increase your salon visibility within the area of location, provide employment opportunities to the qualified people around you. They will help in selling your services through word of mouth. They will refer their friends to your salon and the chain will continue. The community will also feel that the business is not only providing services but also improving the lives of the people.

In conclusion, the community that surrounds you is the reason why your salon exists. Without them you cannot prosper. You need to recognize them and give back to them. This will build strong public relation and customer loyalty.

As I have stated in earlier social media can really help your business grow and it's very cost effective for the brand new and experienced hair stylist. The salon business is heavily competitive and if you are just starting out, you may find it difficult to get clients that's why I am sharing with you social media again. Socializing is the major marketing strategy for a hair stylist. You may have noticed that when you satisfy your clients, they refer others to you and this is how your business grows. Since the world has now gone hi-tech, you can use the internet to your advantage by using online social networking platforms.

Social media marketing for hairstylists offers you the one of the best opportunities to connect with your clients and potential clients. The most popular social networking sites that you can use are Facebook and Twitter. They even allow you to have a greater bond with your clients. If you have not embraced social media marketing, it is the high time for you to consider social networking as a great marketing strategy for your salon business.

How to use Facebook

Facebook is a popular option when it comes to social media marketing for salons. You are on the right track if you have a Facebook account. You can use your Facebook profile to market your hairstylist business or you can create a business page. When conversing with your clients inquire from them if they have Facebook profiles and suggest to them that you would like to become friends. If you have a business profile, you can request them to like your page. You should also make sure that your business cards contain your Facebook information.

When using Facebook to market your business, you should post information that is relevant to your clients. For instance, you can post information about the specials you are currently offering, the best client photos, industry, hair care tips and other information related to your profession. You can also post personal information with discretion. It will allow your clients or potential clients to know you better.

How to use Twitter

Twitter is a simple but fast paced social networking site. After setting up an account, you just need to tell your clients about it and add your Twitter name to your business cards. In order to get the conversation rolling in Twitter, you have to start "talking". Generally, when you follow a person on Twitter, he/she will follow you back. You should therefore start by following your favorite industry websites, companies and publications. When you follow and start conversing with people in your industry, other twitter users will start following you too.

Just like with Facebook, you should post personal and industry information that is relevant to your clients. You can increase the chances of being found by posting information regularly. You can "talk" to twitter users by adding the sign @ before the handle. You can also utilize hashtags by placing the # sign before popular phrases in the hairstylist industry such as # haircolor, # hair, and # hairstyles among others. Such hashtags will assist those who are searching for information about the salon industry to find you.

Taking advantage of social media marketing for salons is a great way to advertise your business. One of the major advantages of social media marketing is that it is not necessary to pay for the service. You can use social networking sites to make any kind of announcement about your salon business and this will drive up your sales. Now I have mentioned a few social media sites in this book but as a hairstylist you really should leverage multiple methods for attracting and retaining clients and customers.

CHARLOTTE HOWARD ~ TRANSFORMATIONAL LIFE COACH & BEAUTY SALON SUCCESS MENTOR

10 STRATEGIES FOR CREATING MORE HAPPINESS IN YOUR LIFE

Charlotte Howard is a world renowned influential multi-international bestseller publishing expert, transformational life coach, philanthropist , energy healer, journalist and beauty salon success mentor.

A successful certified licensed cosmetologist in her early teenage years working over 80 hours per week, Charlotte has hidden her traumatic childhood experiences and mental and physical abuse while still managing to succeed in her professional life. With just a blink of an eye that changed quickly, when she was diagnosed with carpal tunnel syndrome.

Prescribed to evaluate her life, priorities, and challenges from her past, Charlotte saw her diagnosis as an immediate wake-up call that empowered her to create a massive shift in her life. To begin her healing process she emerged herself with prayer, writing and energy healing strategies. As a passion driven cosmetologist, she opened up her heart to the overflow of opportunities presented to her.

Unwilling to undergo mandatory surgery, Charlotte turned to alternative strategies and experienced a tremendous breakthrough while transitioning in her life. While recovering, she realized that her unresolved challenges mentally and physically are exactly what led her to the point of illness she was experiencing.

1. Use Affirmations Effectively

If affirmations don't work for you, consider the fact that you may be investing your energy and hope into (a) unrealistic ones you don't really believe in or (b) generic affirmations that are too vague and broad-ranging.

The key to making affirmations work is two-fold:

Be specific. Take your affirmation from pie-in-the-sky platitude to something you can achieve

Make sure you believe in the message at a gut level

Anyone can say: "I am a millionaire right now", but that is not really an affirmation—it's wishful thinking.

On the other hand, telling yourself daily: "I have a millionaire mindset" can be a powerful boost to your confidence and outlook, if you pair it with a plan of action.

2. Change your Glass

Are you a "glass-half-empty" person? If so, call yourself on these negative, doom-and-gloom self-messages. Say: "Oops, that's a glass-half-empty thought. Let's turn this around and transform this thought into glass-half-full."

It may feel contrived and your heart may not be in this little exercise at first, if you've been undergoing stress or challenges in your business or personal life—but if you persevere, you will soon discover that deliberately changing glass-half-empty thoughts to glass-half-full ones increases:

Gratitude

Empowerment

Optimism

Proactivity

And ultimately—success!

3. Cut Toxic People Out of Your Life

As human beings, we can't help but be influenced by what the people around us say and do. Inevitably, toxic people come into our lives—people who drag us down instead of building us up (or at least, not harming us!) If someone drains you of energy, makes you lose confidence or feel worse about yourself, cut off contact.

This is easier said than done, since we all want to be loved or at least liked. Try applying a checklist.

Ask yourself:

"Does that person...

Talk only about themselves?

Focus solely on what I can do for them?

Make me feel stressed or heavy at the thought of interacting with them?

Suck me into a negative mind-frame?

Make me doubt my abilities?"

If you answered yes to even one of these, time to either change your responses—or cut the cord.

4. Reframe Negative Thoughts

The damage may be done. A negative family environment or significant relationship has left you with poor self-esteem or poor processing habits. Or perhaps it was that toxic company you worked at for twelve years.

But no matter what caused you to adopt an "I'm doomed, I may as well give up: Happiness/success is not for me" head space, you can make the decision to change that—starting today.

One successful technique that psychologists use is called "reframing".

Here's how to do it:

Take a negative, habitual thought

Filter it in an objective manner through the light of reality

Replace your negative thought with a positive but realistic, corrected version

You can do this with any type of thought—business or personal. (For example, change "I always screw up" with: "I don't always screw up. Sometimes I make mistakes, like everybody else—but I learn from them.")

5. Avoid "All-or-Nothing" Thinking

A particular type of highly destructive self-talk is known in psychological circles as "all-or-nothing thinking". To ensure you don't do it, watch out particularly for the words "always" or "never" in self-talk: For example, "I always fail at everything I do" or "I'll never learn how to do split-testing".

All-or-nothing thinking is just another way of beating yourself up, and strips away both personal power and confidence.

If you catch yourself making an all-or-nothing statement, reframe it instantly to a more realistic, empowering thought. (E.g.: "Lots of people learn how to split-test effectively: I can choose to outsource this or I can just take my time, read instructions more carefully—and do it till I get it right.")

6. Avoid Catastrophizing

Are you a catastrophizer? Is every setback that happens the end of the world? Do you scream things like "my business is FINISHED" if your mouse dies, instead of simply changing the battery?

Yes, this is just another form of beating yourself up. Even if you do experience a disaster—for example, a power outage occurs and you lose a graphics file you've been working on for hours—realize that in the large scheme of things, this is frustrating but not really the end of your world.

Treat it as a learning experience. (Example: "Next time I'll remember to save that graphic at every step.")

7. Ask Yourself: "Will This Matter in Five Years?"

One of the best ways to train yourself out of a doom-oriented, catastrophizing head space is to get into the habit of asking yourself, after each disaster: "Will this matter in five years?"

If the answer is "no, I won't even remember it", it's not worth getting in a knot over. As wildly successful entrepreneur E. Joseph Cossman once said: "If you want to test your memory, try to recall what you were worrying about one year ago today."

8. Set a Limit on Worry Time

If you are a chronic worrywart or a particular task or event is causing you to worry, table it. Set aside a specific time to worry (e.g. "I'm going to think about this from 10:15 a.m. to 10:40").

Then when you start to fret about it, tell yourself: "It's not worry time yet—I'll put that aside till later".

9. Realize that Fear is Just Excitement

You may have "learned" that the butterfly-sensation in your stomach before you give a presentation or doing hair for the first time is "fear". Try reframing that to: "Wow, I sure am excited about this!"

Changing fear into excitement in your mind is the first step to taking action, taking risks—and succeeding.

10. Recognize that Feelings May Follow Actions—Not Precede Them

Most people give up too easily when they are attempting to change mental habits. This happens because they expect their feelings to change instantly.

The more negativity or powerlessness is ingrained in our habitual thoughts, the longer it takes to "break" that response. Go through exercises such as reframing anyway and one day before too long, you'll find your feelings will eventually follow.

Wishing you fulfillment and happiness,

Charlotte

DAIJA HOWARD ~ WOMEN LIFE MENTOR & #1 INTERNATIONAL BEST SELLING AUTHOR

10 STRATEGIES FOR ENHANCING YOUR LIFE

Daija Howard, the chief executive editor at Heart Centered Women Publishing and chief executive coordinator for Beaut Lifestyle Women's Mastermind Retreats.

She is the youngest women's life mentor who has edited and contributed to helping over 40 books become international best sellers. For over a decade, Daija has empowered young women of all walks of life on how to increase their self esteem, confidence and achieve anything their heart desires through authentic personal growth and self healing strategies.

1. See Failure as a Learning Opportunity

This is no trite platitude. The most successful entrepreneurs aren't the ones that instantly succeed: They are the ones that get up, take notes of what didn't work, brainstorm—and keep going.

True failure is never trying in the first place.

2. Focus Outward

Our worst worries, fear and paralysis behaviors and mindsets occur when we are focused inward—on ourselves.

Focus outward instead: On how you are going to help the person you are writing that eBook for; or how much it will help not just your client but other members of his team if you get your project in on time.

When we are focused on helping others, there is no room for worry.

3. Find your Passion

Even if you're stuck in a business you can't instantly get out of, look for what you are truly passionate about within it: What in this current business makes time fly, instills you with vision and confidence, and brings satisfaction?

Find a way to tap into that. Tweak your routines, outsource energy-draining tasks—and most important, adjust your overall business plan so that you are more closely following the path that inspires you towards your success goals.

4. Realize that You are Already a Success

You are still in the business of entrepreneurship. You have picked yourself up and dusted yourself off so many times, it has become a habit.

And if you've unsuccessfully tried business model after business model, don't be discouraged. You're in the company of truly great entrepreneurs like Oprah, Sir Richard Branson and Ariana Huffington (whose mother pointed out: "Failure is a stepping stone to success").

Even if you have a string of failures behind you, this only means you've already proven you have the Number One trait of all truly successful entrepreneurs: Tenacity. You never give up.

So keep on keeping on—and congratulate yourself for being on the right track.

5. Avoid Analysis Paralysis

Did you know that over-preparing and over-analyzing can be another form of procrastination—or at the very least, avoidance behavior?

Especially if it is stopping you from branching out or taking any sort of risk.

To get past this, get into the habit of setting cut-off dates. ("On Tuesday the sixteenth, no matter how unprepared I feel, I'm just going to launch this website.")

Giving yourself a definite cut-off date and making a commitment to stick to it can help focus your thinking and spur you into action.

6. Beware of the Feedback Loop

Are you addicted to collecting feedback and opinions before taking each step?

Do you ask everyone in your family, members of your Facebook Group and the membership site you belong to? (If you added "the mailman, my hairstylist friends, my son's two best friends and the family dog", the answer is definitely "yes!")

Cut this number drastically. Pre-select only the people who have given you professionally-valid and knowledgeable advice: Who can be honest without cutting you down—those who provide constructive criticism you can use to improve, rather than those who complain or make you feel like they're taking over your project.

Asking too many people indiscriminately for feedback can actually signal a huge lack of confidence. Limit the number to under half a dozen—and chose them with care. (Think "accountability partner" more than "feedback provider".)

7. Cultivate Self-awareness

Being self-aware doesn't mean beating yourself up or giving yourself negative messages: It means assessing yourself as objectively as you would assess any business idea.

Get into the habit of asking yourself questions like:

What am I doing well?

What do I have trouble with?

What could I do better? How?

What am I doing too much of?

How do my subscribers and followers see me?

How do I see myself?

Done properly, not only can this help you succeed—it's also fun as you uncover each possibility.

8. Learn to Develop Radar

This is a particular component of the self-awareness process: "Radar" occurs when a little alarm bell goes off in your brain or gut, telling you (if you catch it and actually stop to listen to it) that something is either wildly exciting and therefore full of potential/right for you... or completely off-kilter.

Most people are so caught up in worry or activity that they ignore these barely-noticeable frissons—but entrepreneurs count them as invaluable micro-clues to staying on course for success.

9. Be Secretly Organized.

Even the most maverick and cavalier top entrepreneur is secretly organized—even when they come flying into an event by the skin of their teeth. Setbacks and curveballs rarely rattle them because they have set in place systems and habits to deal with every eventuality.

These are the entrepreneurs who always have a "signature" presentation in their pocket for last-minute emergency fill-ins; who employ strong teams to watch their backs; who always leave early to get to events on time; create plans and follow them—while building in flexibility, so they can "go with the flow".

Being organized doesn't mean scheduling yourself down to the last second of your day: It means being prepared for more than one scenario and giving yourself the freedom to think on the fly.

10. Act on the Short Stuff

Reduce overwhelm by doing any task that is going to take less than five minutes immediately.

You'll feel much more relaxed and accomplished by the end of the day.

To your total lifestyle enhancement,

Daija

SONYA DAVIS ~ BEAUTY INDUSTRY EXPERT & #1 INTERNATIONAL BEST SELLING AUTHOR

10 STRATEGIES FOR ENHANCING YOUR CAREER AND BUSINESS

Sonya Davis is an accomplished beauty industry expert, author, speaker and leading image consultant. She trains and "EMPOWERS" families worldwide on how to enhance their lives mentally, physically, spiritually and financially. As an international best selling author, paralegal and spiritual ambassador, she uses her god given talents to help others achieve their goals.

Discover her authentic lessons through her #1 International Best Selling Book Success In Beauty: The Secrets To Confidently Following Your Dreams Effortlessly, New Hope Horizon Baptist Church where she co-pastors and her signature Beaut Lifestyle Women Retreats. Contact her today to Claim your FREE "Reinvent Your Lifestyle" membership guaranteed to help you create a total life change.

1. Change your Environment

Getting tired? Feeling stale? If so, try changing your environment— not just by going for a walk or doing a little gardening, but physically taking your work to another location.

Work on the patio during summertime. Try an internet café during colder seasons.

And if you're doing heavy research—base yourself in your local library. (Not only will your mind be stimulated by the change of scene, you'll have extra resources at your fingertips.)

2. Know your Triggers

If you find yourself procrastinating, don't worry so much about the cause: Find your triggers. What sends you into Avoidance-Land? Is it a particular topic you have to write about? The fact that you hate bookkeeping or cleaning house? A particularly unpleasant client? One that reminds you of that scary fifth grade teacher?

Sometimes when we identify causes and triggers, we are able to deflate the bogeyman. ("Hey, I'm not ten years old any more. So what if this client talks like her?") And there are other actions you can take: For example, hire a cleaning lady once or twice a week if you hate housework or outsource your salon bookkeeping to a bookkeeper.

Most important, however: Recognizing and naming a trigger takes away its power. We then feel empowered to make proactive choices and deal with what is making us want to put off a task or responsibility.

3. Reward yourself

This isn't a new concept—yet too many entrepreneurs seem to forget about it due to worrying and focusing on business necessities.

The most successful entrepreneurs, however, know how to enjoy the perks of the entrepreneur lifestyle.

Choose yours carefully and fit them in. (So you can't afford a weekend at a luxury resort right now—but maybe you can invest in a "reading afternoon" or a bunch of fresh flowers every weekend.)

When you see tangible evidence of your hard work bring about a reward, it is much easier to feel balanced, accomplished, happier—and more confident. So consider this a necessary business investment!

4. Set Ground Rules—for Yourself!

If you constantly find yourself reactively responding to family or friends who don't seem to understand you are working, set ground rules: Not just for your nearest and dearest, but for yourself. For example, set work hours and tell the worst offenders you won't be available during that time period every day. Then respect your own rules if they call or "drop in".

Don't answer the door. Don't pick up the phone if you see their names on Call Display. Don't answer emails or Facebook PMs.

If you stick to your guns, they will eventually realize you mean what you say: But if you make exceptions, you've only yourself to blame when they turn up on your doorstep during work hours. (If you don't respect yourself and your clients, they won't!)

5. Identify your Weak Points—and Plan Around them

Knowing your weaknesses is the first step to managing—and overcoming—their negative effects. The key is to identify them without judging yourself.

For example, if you know that you will procrastinate all day if you start the morning with Facebook, rearrange your schedule so that you do an hour of solid work first before checking your Facebook feeds.

6. Break it Down into Bite-sized Chunks

This is especially true for any task that overwhelms you or makes you procrastinate. If the thought of writing a thirty-page eBook has you running to clean the silverware, just so you won't have to face it, then break that task down into "baby steps".

Set daily goals that are easily manageable, no matter how overwhelmed you feel: For example, writing 500 words a day, or one page a day.

7. Use Apps, Schedulers and Timers to Help Manage your Workload

Find out where you need help, and use apps, schedulers or timers as memory prompts or incentives to help you manage your workload— as well as important life tasks such as: "Take morning pills!" or "Time to drink another glass of water".

8. Learn to Delegate

Make the most of family, friends and employees who love to do tasks you hate. Delegate tasks that drain your energy.

And don't forget to thank and reward those who help you out.

9. Plan for Outsourcing

Whether you are in the salon behind the chair or in the office. No one can do everything (even though many people pretend they do). Top entrepreneurs always have top teams—of fellow specialists/professionals to whom they delegate or outsource non-money-making tasks.

(And you can outsource personal life tasks too!)

10. Listen

When so much emphasis is on doing, achieving, producing in the entrepreneurial landscape, many entrepreneurs forget to really stop and listen.

Listen to your customers and clients. Listen to your followers. Listen to your peers—and especially to your team.

Make notes of things that strike you (it's guaranteed you may not remember them later, if you don't). Follow up on things promised or concerns expressed.

The most successful people know how to listen—and follow through.

Wishing you much abundance,

Sonya

SUCCESS STORIES

Every time you find yourself particularly enjoying something—anything at all, from taking a simple but refreshing nap every afternoon to the Adrenalin rush of creating your first six-figures in the beauty industry—get into the habit of asking yourself: "How can I create more of this?"

In order to create more of something, you need to let go of something else; so the second part of this question is: "How do I get rid of ...?"

In order to create more of what you want, you need to focus on it, live it, breathe it—and plan for more. It doesn't just happen on its own. So go after what you love—and what makes you feel excited to be alive.

Finally, realize that these mind-hacks are not something you "should" do. Pick and choose, adapting them to your personality and goals. They are here for you to pick up and use, like instruments, so you can fine-tune your business and your life to finally create true happiness and success.

In every issue of Hairstylist Riches, I will feature beauty industry experts and business owners from all walks of life. I hope you enjoy their unique strategies and heart felt stories to be an inspiration during your beauty industry journey.

Cheers,

Charlotte

ALAN BENFIELD BUSH ~ INTERNATIONAL HAIR ICON

METHOD ALLIANCE ~ TRANSFORMING SALON INDUSTRY EDUCATION!

Alan Benfield Bush: As one of the most recognized educators and motivational speakers in the professional salon industry, Bush has received many awards for his educational presentations and formula-based teaching methods. Bush is best known for this Method that has been previously shared internationally with Vidal Sassoon Academy, Paul Mitchell Haircare and his own company. His primary focus remains to touch the lives and hearts of hair design engineers using his advanced education techniques. Bush remains sincerely dedicated to help hairstylists improve their artistic skills and business acumen.

Why I Got Into The Professional Beauty Industry: "I started to be intrigued when I began going to the local town barber shop. I found a great atmosphere, from the fragrances, the laughter and all of the dirty jokes; and so I felt very comfortable.

How The Beauty Industry Changed My Life: "The professional salon industry gave me a sense of direction that I never had before. I really liked that it was not just a short-term job! It offered me a career where I could be paid well if I worked hard. I was also influenced by the Vidal Sassoon era of contemporary haircuts and creative hair designs. In 1964, I opened two barber shops and one beauty salon. I am proud to say that my original partner still has the beauty salon open today. The beauty industry has also changed my life by helping me understand that it is my mission to help hairdressers improve their economics and artistic skills."

How The Beauty Industry Changed My Life: "The professional salon industry gave me a sense of direction that I never had before. I really liked that it was not just a short-term job! It offered me a career where I could be handsomely paid. I also got successfully attracted to the Vidal Sassoon era of contemporary haircuts and creative hair designs. In 1965, I opened two barber shops and one beauty salon. I am proud to say that my original partner still has the beauty salon open today. The beauty industry has also changed my life by helping me understand that it is my mission to help others successfully change their careers and lives."

What I Love Most About Our Salon Industry: "I love making people happy and inspired! I love making people feel good about themselves! This certainly includes my models, clients and every salon industry professional that I work with."

Strategies For Experts To Enhance Your Lives, Career & Business With Confidence: "Make sure that you continue to get plenty of advanced, generic education. Learn about the art and craft; not biased by the too much manufacturer and product-based education. Search for top salon industry educators and events that are independent and not directly associated with product manufacturers. For example, as Ryan Teal quoted: "Mario Andretti does not go to Marlboro to learn how to drive a race car." Advanced education is not a one-time-a-year event. Keep yourself updated on the latest services, haircutting and business techniques throughout the year, by a wide variety of resources!"

"We have recently established the new Method Alliance Hair Icons Team. We are dedicated to empower the hairdresser while featuring generic business and technical education with The Method, using a universal approach to length, width and depth. Whether you are a traditional salon owner, a hairstylist or an independent solo hair designer, you need to continually advance your career with ongoing advanced education. It is very important to attend as many local and national professional beauty shows and educational events as possible. Take the time to subscribe to magazines, websites and Internet connections that will share advanced educational events, advice and tips."

"Promote your service specialties, certifications and advanced skills to continually build your client's confidence in you. Keep a visual record of every client's makeovers, to share the diversity of your skills, since you will always have a diverse clientele with differing needs. Display photographs of your best makeovers and service work on Facebook, social media, your website, via email blasts and in a professional portfolio within your work station or salon suite area. Send your photographs with brief articles about your advanced skills and certifications to the local media."

Manage Your Clientele: "You must already have a loyal repeat clientele. You need to be ready to train your clientele. You should educate and train each client to become your spokesperson and salespeople, so they can help tell others, work associates and the local media about your specialties, expertise and service qualities. They can easily help promote you in social media today, besides the normal word-of-mouth referrals.

Be ready to develop and institute a strongly promoted New Client Referral Rewards Program that is also a V.I.P. Rewards Program for your best clients. Make sure your Rewards Program is a true win-win for the new clients as well as for your regulars. While every client can help, you only need three or four good clients to primarily represent you within the community.

Print salon service menus, business cards and Referral Reward Program devices that can be shared with them and their connections. Offer valuable free services to your regulars that can be earned and used throughout the next year. Tell them that if they send you enough new clients, they can possibly earn a free year of haircare services."

Whether you own a salon, work in a traditional salon or work independently, you will need to continually learn about all of the advantages, challenges, pitfalls and opportunities. Take control! Be ready to become a marketer of your salon services, products, specialties and total business, so you can grow from your loyal client base to build an ever-expanding client base. Both new client recruitment and client retention are very important factors. Your marketing, PR and promotional activities will be more important than your current client retention. If you are building more new clients than the number leaving you each year, you are not in control. Do what you do best. If you are not a marketer, a publicist or a graphic designer, hire someone with those talents."

The Method: Alan Benfield Bush is best known for inventing a revolutionary different and trademarked system of haircutting called "The Method." This system is a universally accepted language tool. Bush notes, "The Method educational workshops utilize the English language to properly describe the science of designing hair."

Alan Benfield Bush authored the much respected Condensed Cutting Technique, Condensed Perm Technique, Condensed Colour Technique and Condensed Setting Technique. He has taught design within the architectural art form and has mentored The Method to hairstylists across the globe. The Method has three forms of haircutting called geometrics, volumetrics and trimetric projections.

The Method helps bring salon professionals together on a level of understanding of the elements that we all use to create professional hair designs. With The Method techniques, hair designers quickly become the master in control of their own creativity and their career. Bush promises, "Mastering The Method will give you the ultimate freedom with hair design creativity!"

Method Alliance ~ Offering Creative New Hair Design & Business Solutions: Bush notes, "My life-long passion has turned a dream into a reality with the launch of the Method Alliance as a new educationally based company. Our team provides valuable hair artistry and generic business education for salon industry professionals, without promoting any specific haircare brands. These innovative new educational programs have been developed expressly for hair design engineers, salon owners, distributors and manufacturers. The Method Alliance has quickly gained respectability from top salon owners, hair design engineer, manufacturers and distributors."

The Method Alliance provides workshops that are customized for hair designers, manufacturers and distributors. Besides teaching creative hair design artistry, many programs help improve your business skills with profitable performance techniques. They are ready to support you with in-salon hands-on training programs, telephone consulting services, DVD/videos and webinars, starting with The Method and their newest innovative two-day Cutoloring Workshops. All educational programs will benefit licensed salon professionals and cosmetology students. The Method Alliance Company offers ongoing coaching, consulting and education with annual retainer-based programs to ensure your long-term success.

Method Alliance ~ Hair Icons Team: Bush adds, "I am very proud of the shared energies by this new educational platform artistry team of fantastic internationally respected hair designers!" The Method Alliance Hair Icons Team provides valuable hair artistry and generic business education for artistic engineers, salon owners, distributors and manufacturers. This includes an innovative non-branded and 100% generic approach. Besides teaching creative hair design, they also have programs to improve business skills with profitable techniques. Our team currently includes Allan Ngo, Chad Clark, Angel del Solar, Alexander Baron, J Christian Gallagher and Hector Rodriguez."

M.A.T.E. Bush shares, "We also launched the 'Method Alliance Transforming Education' organization to support all hair design engineers. For those who strive to take their career to the next level; M.A.T.E. will help members learn how to become successful educators and platform artists for regional and national education programs. They will learn how to teach The Method with advanced level training through workshops, video-taped auditions and photography sessions. Each certified M.A.T.E team member receives a plaque to recognize their abilities."

MARC FINER ~ TRANSFORM YOUR CAREER WITH A SUITE NEW VISION

TURN YOUR BURNOUT INTO A NEW BEGINNING FOR YOUR SALON OR SPA CAREER

Marc Finer has over 30 years in the beauty industry with a diverse background in international sales, retail and marketing. He takes great pride that he envisioned salon suite rental as the fastest growing new salon concept of the future -- a paradigm shift in the beauty industry. His next biggest accomplishment was being able to see it to fruition with the creation and development of a unique concept dedicated to the proposition that not all beauty professionals are created equal! Through six locations with over 150 tenants, he has seen first-hand what this suites concept will successfully accomplish. Helping others achieve success, inspires Finer to do more.

Why I Got Into The Professional Beauty Industry: Marc Finer shares, "I fell upon the potential future salon suite concept in its infancy stage many years ago and immediately understood it to be the next big thing in the salon industry. I knew it would be a groundbreaking opportunity for experienced salon and spa professionals to discover creative and financial freedoms!"

How The Beauty Industry Changed My Life: "I worked for many years in the retail beauty business. For my family and me, the professional beauty industry opened the door to exciting entrepreneurship and a meaningful career with a rewarding new path for life. With my wife working by my side, our journey parallels that of the health and beauty professionals who break into independence by being confident, taking risks and working around the ever-present obstacles. We are very proud to be part of the paradigm shift in the beauty industry."

What I Love Most About Our Salon Industry: "What I love most about the salon industry is its continual evolution, the creativity and free spirited nature of the licensed professionals who make up its roots."

Strategies For Experts To Enhance Your Lives, Career & Business With Confidence: "Even though an independent beauty career is not for everyone that is licensed to touch, there are many salon and spa professionals who seek a break-through or resurgence today. The salon and spa suite rental concept provides just the right amount of entry level entrepreneurship to make it comfortable, affordable and appealing.

We must all take note of the rapidly growing national trend with salon and spa suites. Recent research shows that one-third of all salon and spa professionals are now working independently. This trend is expected to be 50% of the industry by 2020. Experienced professionals with a loyal clientele are always the most successful at working independently.

As long as you know all of the facts, there are many strategic advantages to enhance your career and life in a salon or spa suite. You will instantly become your own boss! You will have 100% control of your earnings, income and career. Salon suites are perfect for hair designers, barbers, aestheticians, nailcare and makeup artists as well as all massage and spa professionals. Unlike traditional salons, a salon suite provides the opportunity for established busy salon and spa professionals with a clientele to break free from their commissioned structure and limited freedoms working for someone else. It is important to note that you will still need to be licensed and pay taxes, like any salon or spa owner.

Rediscover Your Passion: The Phoenix is a mythical firebird with the ability to be reborn out of its own ashes. The brightly plumed bird ignites into flame, only to rise again in a never-ending cycle of rebirth. The story of the sacred bird is a wonderful symbol for renewal and second chances. Just like the Phoenix, we can all turn our burnout into an opportunity for a positive new transformation.

The professional beauty industry remains a very exciting career path, with many diverse directions available to you, from owning or working in traditional salons to exploring all of the independent options. No matter your professional category, salon and spa suites are now changing the way professionals live and work. Salon and spa suites are the perfect way to find a new beginning, by adding exciting new freedom and flexibility to your career and life!

Salon and spa professionals often experience burnout working in a traditional salon or in any working capacity. Career burnout may take the form of irritation, fatigue, apathy, lack of interest in work or even physical illness. Realizing you need a change is just the beginning to building a new foundation and vision for work or life. Today, you can rise like the Phoenix from your current challenges to start fresh. The first step is simply to ask what your life could look like if you allowed yourself to change direction. If you are challenged by fear, anger, sadness or jealousy, use those strong feelings to ignite your passion for a new beginning.

The Suite Life With No Limits: Imagine your life without limits. Imagine earning the income you desire, working the hours you want, and achieving the dreams you believed in when you first started your beauty career. Having your own business within Salonz Beauty & Spa Suites offers you an instant opportunity with a minimal investment and no long-term commitments, so you can get started right away. You will be able to create your own work schedule and come and go as you please, 7 days a week, 365 days a year. Some of the many salon suite facilities contain unique advantages. Salonz Beauty & Spa Suites layouts for example, allow you the flexibility to be private with your clients, or open for walk-ins and socializing with your neighbors. Renting a salon suite allows you to set your own prices, and to select your favorite services and retail products to sell, while independently controlling all of the money you earn.

Success With Suite Advantages: This rapidly expanding concept is successfully raging across the country. At Salonz, each suite includes all utilities, Wi-Fi, and telephone and cable TV jacks. In addition, your name and business information will be posted on the lobby directory and next to your suite door, your business cards and brochures will be presented in the elegant lobby for regular and walk-in clients, you will be provided with postcards and referral cards to reach current and potential clients, and you will have access to free educational and marketing seminars, and workshops throughout the year. At Salonz Beauty & Spa Suites you are independent, not alone!

Discover The Best Options For You! The primary benefit of being a suite renter is the freedom it offers to be your own boss, but you must also understand the challenges. Not all beauty professionals are ready to rent a suite. Many still favor the comfort of a traditionally structured environment, working on a commission basis. In addition, newly licensed professionals or those without a strong client base should not rent a suite until they are better established. By the same token, even if someone does have a large clientele, they may not have the self-discipline or initiative to run their own business. Salonz Beauty & Spa Suites is interested in seeing their tenants succeed, and work hard to help promote their businesses and grow their careers.

There are two types of salon and spa suite models; company-owned and franchised. Both offer the same basic amenities, equipment and rent ranges. The company-owned models are typically more experienced, knowledgeable and service-oriented.

They have built their concept from the ground up, having learned through trial and error. The company-owned models are also likely to be owned by persons from a related beauty, retail or customer service industry, while franchised facilities are typically owned by people who are unrelated to the beauty business and without any direct salon or spa experience. In addition, the company-owned model is typically owned by a local operator who knows and understands the market and demographics.

In contrast, with little or no grass roots knowledge of the concept or the salon industry, the franchisee typically yields to the franchisor, who is most often situated in another part of the country with no local knowledge.

Finally, the company-owned suite business owner, given their grass roots, operational experience, is more likely able to react quicker to challenges and manage each tenant situation effectively. A potential benefit of a franchised model is name recognition, although that doesn't necessarily translate into better operational efficiency to help the tenants meet their personal and career goals.

New & Positive Turnkey Business Opportunities: Do you like the sound of working for yourself and being paid to do what you love? It can be a reality! Salon beauty suites are making dreams come true for health and beauty professionals. So many beauty professionals are not happy where they are. After years of hard work, many dream of owning their own salon but the investment and hassle make it impossible. Now for a minimal cost, salon suite concepts will help set up professionals in their own businesses.

Where your clients are concerned, a principal goal is to have a diverse tenant mix. With all services offered in one location; clients can be taken care of from head to toe! This is the hottest trend to hit the salon industry, and is the best of all worlds...offering health and beauty professionals the ability to express their talents with their own unique style, in their own personalized suites. Salonz tenants are doing what they love ... and on their terms. Like the beautiful Phoenix, rediscover your professional career in beauty to reignite the passion that got you started in this industry in the first place!"

LARRY OSKIN ~ MARKETING SOLUTIONS

SALON & SPA MARKETING SPECIALISTS

Larry H. Oskin: Oskin is president of Marketing Solutions, the leading marketing, branding, advertising, PR, social media and consulting services agency specializing in the professional salon, spa, medical and beauty businesses. He is a creative beauty industry executive with over 40 years of professional marketing and management experiences. Oskin has been published as a beautycare marketing expert in hundreds of consumer and trade publications.

Oskin is often referred to as a "Marketing ChangeMaster" and a "Guerrilla Marketeer". Marketing Solutions works with every level of the professional beauty business, inclusive of salons, day spas, wellness centers, medical spas, cosmetic surgeons, medical clinics, salon chains, manufacturers, distributors and associations from across North America. The Marketing Solutions Team always creates `customized education-based strategic marketing programs' to meet each client's distinctively unique and special needs. As a sister company, Art Beautique offers creative fine art photography services for salons, spas and beautycare businesses.

Why & How I Got Into The Professional Beauty Industry: "I first worked in advertising, marketing, graphic design, photography and PR for a large advertising agency in Buffalo, New York handling real estate, bank, supermarket, retail, automobile and service industry accounts. After national recognition and publicity from when I helped convert a large chain of grocery stores to supermarkets, I was invited to join America's largest national beauty salon chain – Steppes Beauticians. Their challenge was for me to help them be the first in the United States to become a new national chain of unisex hair salons. We successfully opened Hair Happening, Shear Happening Salons and the very first JC Penney Salons.

After 5 years, Steppes Beauticians' salon chain was sold to Regis Corporation, a smaller beauty salon chain. I joined Regis! As a vice president, I helped manage all of their marketing, branding, advertising, pricing, PR, photography, retail products, manufacturer relations, promotions and education – just as I had done for Steppes.

We took Regis to become respected as the world's largest publically held salon chain. After that, I was Vice President of the Ratner Companies with Hair Cuttery and Bubbles Salon organization, before opening my own Marketing Solutions agency business in 1992."

How The Beauty Industry Changed My Life: "The professional salon industry changed my career and life! I have been fortunate to work with hair designers, salon and spa professionals from across the globe. I actively work with manufacturers, distributors, salon chains and beautycare entrepreneurs from small start-ups to major international businesses. The beauty industry allowed me to live in numerous states as well as to travel across the globe.

The salon industry has opened many new doors for me while allowing me to make many, many life-long friendships. I have been able to personally work with Myron Kunin, Vidal Sassoon, Tom Peters, Angus Mitchell, Alan Benfield Bush, Jim Markham, Ian Gavet and many other notable beauty industry hair icons. I have also had fun working with many beauty pageant title holders as well as other Hollywood and TV celebrities. I have been invited to speak at numerous salon and spa conventions across the globe on marketing, branding and PR strategies."

What I Love Most About Our Salon Industry: "I really love the professional beauty and fashion industry as it is very creative, artistic, global and ever-changing!"

Marketing Strategies For Experts To Enhance Your Lives, Career & Business With Confidence: "Every individual salon and spa professional must create an annual marketing and branding strategy for yourself, your business and for your career. Here are some tips and ideas to meet your strategic goals and objectives:

- **Annual Marketing Calendars:** Start a calendar to determine which service and products you want to promote on a bi-monthly basis, using 6 two-month promotional periods per year. Take into account all of the holidays and seasons, like New Year – New Year Makeovers, Valentine's Day, Mother's Day, Father's Day, Halloween and the Year-End Holidays.

- **Salon Service Brochure:** Make sure it has your logo, name, photographs, a list of your specialty services, phone, email, Facebook page and website. Make it consistent with your special branded colors.

- **Network With An Email List:** Start to collect the names, emails and birthdays of your clients, so you can send out a monthly email blast.

- **Monthly / B-Monthly Email Blasts:** Use your Marketing Calendar to plan an ongoing series of email blasts.

- **Website:** Work with a local resource to develop a professional website to promote yourself and your business. Add biographies, makeover photographs, a complete salon service menu with prices and your list of retail products.

- **Social Media & Facebook:** Post weekly and monthly updates for your advanced education updates with new certifications, your promotions, seasonal specials and events.

- **Special Days & Open House Events:** This is a great way to get your regulars to bring in their families and friends. Offer free lecture demonstrations, door prizes and refreshments.

- **Birthday Cards:** Share a personalized Birthday Wish by email or mail with a free product, sample or discount offered on their next services.

- **Special Retail Promotions:** Work with your manufacturers and distributors to offer seasonal retail promotions. Ask them to share their free retail marketing devices.

- **YouTube Video Series:** Start a series of videos to show off your service specialties, while teaching your clients how to take care of their hair, skin, nails and image between salon and spa visits.

- **Charitable Events:** Whether you do it alone or with others; participate in Cut-A-Thons, Spa-A-Thons, Nail-A-Thons or whatever you can do to help those less fortunate. Select and work with recognized local and national charities.

- **Community Events, Fashion Shows & Bridal Fairs:** Participate in fashion shows, lecture demonstrations and community events to show off your talents. Have plenty of posters and brochures. Have everyone register to win a free door prize, while collecting their names, email addresses and contact information.

- **Full-Price Service Promotions:** Create some seasonal promotions – offering the benefits of your services at full-price.

- **Offer Special Discounts:** Create a series of discounted, gift with service or purchase with purchase promotions.

- **Raise Prices:** Try to adjust your prices 5% per year or 10% every two years.

- **Promote Gift Certificates:** Promote Gift Certificates for holidays and all year long! Develop a Corporate Gifting Program for local businesses and medical centers. Offer "Buy Any $100 Gift Certificate – Get A Bonus FREE $20 Gift Certificate!"

- **Start A Loyalty Program:** Plan to reward your clients for every 10 visits or specialty hair, skin, nail and spa services.

- **New First-Time Client Business Cards:** With a special

welcome using '$10 Off, Half-Price or FREE Service' incentive.

- **Client Referral Club Program:** Develop an aggressive program to reward your current clients and their friends / family with discounts for new first-time clients.

- **Goodie Bags For New First-Time Clients:** With samples and bounce back gift certificates towards services and retail products.

- **Annual PR Program:** Develop a Media Kit with a series of press releases to the local and national consumer media. Send your press releases to the national beauty trade media. Use PR to educate the community, while enhancing your special services and products.

- **Powerful Media Kits For Your Beauty Business:** Create a Media Kit with your Salon or Spa Business Story, your Biography Page, a series of targeted Press Releases, high resolution Photographs and PR Reprints. Your Business Story will be an important part of your backgrounder information to explain the background, purpose and plans for your business – while detailing what makes your beautycare business so unique and different. Your Biography Page will explain what you are expert at, what you specialize in, your successful business accomplishments and all of your accolades.

- **Facilitate PR Photography Sessions:** Plan at least one or two professional photography sessions per year. The media prefers to have photography illustrations with every PR submission. Share photographs with every press release. Use high resolution digital photographs that are 300 dpi or larger. Low resolution, iPhone and stock photographs are not acceptable. If you attend any event or get certified with advanced education, get photographs of yourself with known industry leaders. Use these images to promote yourself and your expertise.

- **Call Clients & Send Thank You Notes:** Call each client after each visit, especially after any special chemical or specialty service. Send Thank You Cards. Send "I Miss You!" Cards to any client who has not made an appointment in 3 or 4 months, with a $20 discount on their next service of $35 / $50 or more.

- **ALWAYS Dress For Respect:** You are your brand! You must be a walking billboard. If you specialize in haircolor, hair extensions, makeup or nailcare; then look the part of a beautycare professional. Be ready to hand out your special New First-Time Client Welcome business cards.

Hire Professionals: If needed, work with a local agency or with a nationally respected beautycare marketing, branding, social media and PR specialist."

Art Beautique: Larry Oskin launched Art Beautique as a new creative fine art photography service and a virtual art gallery specializing in the professional salon, spa and medical industries. Salon and spa owners have been challenged with how to creatively decorate their facilities while also professionally promoting their services – many of which are hidden behind closed doors. There now is a beautiful new solution with Art Beautique Images!

The Art Beautique Collection celebrates the beauty of women, flowers, cityscapes, salon and spa services. Through a special photo impressionism technique, Art Beautique images actually look like impressionistic paintings, using bright, bold and vivid colors.

Art Beautique offers customized opportunities to create special original artwork for salon, spas and medical facilities while turning your professional photography into beautiful one-of-a-kind original artwork by using photo impressionism techniques. Oskin is also available to photograph your facility, services and models. Turn each photography session into original artwork to decorate your walls as well as for a complete photography gallery for marketing, PR and social media.

RESOURCES

CHARLOTTE HOWARD ~ HAIR ARTIST ASSOCIATION & SUCCESS & BEAUTY TALK RADIO SHOW

Contact information: For more information about Charlotte Howard, Hair Artist Association and Success & Beauty Talk Radio Show, contact her at 803-414-2117, email charlotte@thehairartistassociation.org or visit www.thehairartistassociation.org

DAIJA HOWARD ~ HEART CENTERED WOMEN MEDIA, Publishing & TV

Contact information: For more information about Daija Howard, Heart Centered Women Media, Publishing & TV, contact her at 843-376-9044, email heartcenterewomenmedia@gmail.com or visit www.heartcenteredwomenmedia.com

SONYA DAVIS ~ BEAUT LIFESTYLE

Contact information: For more information about Sonya Davis, Beaut Lifestyle Women Mastermind Retreats, contact her at 843-376-9044, email info@thehairartistassociation.org or visit www.BeautLifestyle.com

LARRY OSKIN ~ MARKETING SOLUTIONS

Contact information: For more information about Larry Oskin, Marketing Solutions and Art Beautique, contact Oskin at 407-395-9007. 703-508-6800 or email: LOskin@MktgSols.com. Visit www.ArtBeautique.com and www.MktgSols.com.

ALAN BENFIELD BUSH ~ METHOD ALLIANCE

Contact information: For more information about Bush and Method Alliance regional educational seminars, manufacturer, distributor and special educational events, contact Alan Benfield Bush at 707-217-2700, email Alan@MethodAlliance.com or visit www.MethodAlliance.com.

MARC FINER ~ SALON SPA & SUITES

Contact information: Salonz Beauty & Spa Suites now has six convenient South Florida locations in Boca Raton, Hollywood, Pembroke Pines, Plantation, Palm Beach Gardens and Miami. For more information, a confidential free tour or to reserve your space, call Marc Finer and the Salonz Team at 954-447-1412 or email info@SalonzBeautySuites.com or visit www.SalonzBeautySuites.com

www.ingramcontent.com/pod-product-compliance
Lightning Source LLC
Chambersburg PA
CBHW060548100426
42742CB00013B/2490